Director's Manual

Jesus, Should I Follow You?

Joseph Paprocki
Author

Kieran Sawyer, S.S.N.D.
General Editor

Michael Amodei
Series Editor

Developing Faith
A Mini-Course Series for Teens

AVE MARIA PRESS Notre Dame, Indiana 46556

Nihil Obstat:
Reverend Michael G. Witczak
Censor Liborum

Imprimatur:
The Most Reverend Rembert G. Weakland, O.S.B., D.D.
Archbishop of Milwaukee

Given at Milwaukee, WI on 10 October 1995

The *Nihil Obstat* and *Imprimatur* are official declarations that a book or pamphlet is free of doctrinal or moral error. No implication is contained therein that those who have granted the *Nihil Obstat* and *Imprimatur* agree with its contents, opinions, or statements expressed.

Some of the material in this book was previously published in *Developing Faith* by Sister Kieran Sawyer, copyright © 1978 by Ave Maria Press, Notre Dame, Indiana, *The Jesus Difference* by Sister Kieran Sawyer, copyright © 1987 by Ave Maria Press, Notre Dame, Indiana, and *The Risk of Faith* by Sister Kieran Sawyer, copyright © 1988 by Ave Maria Press, Notre Dame, Indiana.

Scripture passages taken from *The New American Bible with Revised New Testament*, copyright © 1986 by the Confraternity of Christian Doctrine, Washington, D.C., All rights reserved.

© 1996 by Ave Maria Press, Inc.

All rights reserved. No part of this book may be used or reproduced in any manner whatsoever except for materials apppearing on pages labeled for resources; and except in the case of reprints in the context of reviews.

International Standard Book Number: 0-87793-556-4

Cover and text design by Proof Positive/Farrowlyne Associates, Inc.

Printed and bound in the United States of America.

Photography: Jean-Claude Lejeune 22, 31, 32, 42; Gail Denham 65, 104; Luke Golobitsh 54; James L. Shaffer 5, 84, 93; Skjold Photography 73; Jim and Mary Whitmer, 21.

Contents

Welcome	4
Introduction	5
The *Developing Faith* Series in a Complete Faith Development Program	6
About the *Developing Faith* Series	7
How to Use the *Developing Faith* Series in a Complete Faith Development Program	11
Orientation Meeting	19
Mentor Information Meeting	20
Group Sessions	29
Session One Jesus, Should I Follow You?	30
Session Two Jesus, Can I Get to Know You Better?	40
Session Three Jesus, What Do You Stand For?	52
Session Four Jesus, When Do You Speak to Me?	63
Session Five Jesus, What Do You Do For Me?	72
Session Six Jesus, What Am I to Do?	83
Session Seven Jesus, Are You With Me Now?	92
Session Eight Jesus, Am I Ready to Follow You?	103
Appendix	113
Tear-Out Resource Section	123

Welcome

Dear Partners in Religious Education and Youth Ministry,

For years religious educators and youth ministers across the country have been asking me for an entire program based on the methodology found in my *Confirming Faith* sacramental preparation program and the *Tyme Capsule* retreat materials.

The *Developing Faith* mini-course series is an attempt to respond to that plea. Ave Maria Press has gathered a group of top-grade authors and youth practitioners to design with me a program for Catholic-Christian teens that will be engaging, comprehensive, flexible, and theologically sound, and that will involve the entire parish community in supporting the faith development of its adolescent members. I think you will find that a *Developing Faith* mini-course meets each of these criteria:

- Each course includes many dynamic interactive processes designed to *engage* teens' minds and hearts in thoughtful reflection, discussion, and prayer.
- The scope of the series is broad. *Developing Faith* offers mini-courses in all the crucial areas of religious literacy and formation. Enrichment and elective themes add to its *comprehensiveness*.
- The *flexibility* of the series is that it is made up of eight session courses that can be utilized in a variety of times and places in high school religious or youth ministry programs. A complete and easy-to-implement model for a parish faith development program has been provided.
- *Developing Faith* is *theologically sound*. Each course provides solid content in one or more aspects of the Catholic faith as outlined in the *Catechism of the Catholic Church*.

And finally, the *Developing Faith* mini-course series is built on the premise that the faith of adolescents grows best within a caring **faith community** made up of both youth and adults. The processes outlined in the program will help to form the teens and participating adults—catechists, group moderators, mentors, and parents—into a community that is truly Christian.

I encourage you to use the materials in this program creatively, courageously, and prayerfully. The transmission of the Christian faith from one generation to the next is a challenging and mysterious task, one in which God plays a much larger role than any of us. Let us pray together that the seeds of faith, planted at baptism in the hearts of our teens, will develop steadily and surely toward the fullness of Christian life.

Sincerely in Christ,

Sister Kieran Sawyer, SSND

Introduction

The *Developing Faith* Series in a Complete Faith Development Program

The *Developing Faith* series is designed to be the catechetical centerpiece of a comprehensive and flexible faith development program to, for, and by adolescents.

What is meant by a comprehensive and flexible faith development program? In general it is a program that mirrors much of the lifestyle of its participants. It is a program that can roll with a demanding teen schedule that might include basketball practice, a homecoming dance, and driver's training all in one week—yet still claim its rightful place of importance. (A comprehensive and flexible faith development program can likewise meet the varied interests and equally demanding schedules of adults who are asked to serve as catechists, as spiritual partners, and in other volunteer positions.) It is a program with lots of opportunities for free choices and various options. It is a program that recognizes that a fourteen-year-old ninth grader is developmentally much different than an eighteen-year-old senior. A comprehensive and flexible faith development program has many components—not just one or two. Evangelization, welcome, hospitality, prayer, worship, justice, service, mentoring, guidance, building relationships (among all members of the faith community, young and old), and fun are among its parts.

Why a comprehensive and flexible faith development program? A successful program must meet the needs of all its participants. As a consequence, a comprehensive and flexible faith development program offers *many* different times and places to attend, *many* ways to participate, *many* choices, and the opportunity for each person to freely decide what it is he or she needs and would like to learn, do, and be.

What is unique about the *Developing Faith* series? As the vehicle of religious education, the catechetical component of a comprehensive and flexible faith development program is of primary importance. The *Developing Faith* series offers courses in crucial areas of religious literacy and formation, including the scriptures, sacraments, and morality. However, its uniqueness is in its process. The material in *Developing Faith* includes the various kinds of activities that make up a successful faith development program—theological input, dialogue techniques, faith sharing, prayer experience, service opportunities, intergenerational participation—within each of the eight two to two-and-one-half hour sessions. Hence, participants in this *Jesus, Should I Follow You?* mini-course experience in miniature the totality of a comprehensive and flexible faith development program.

The flexibility of the *Developing Faith* series also lends itself to many other faith-developing situations for adolescents. In part or whole, the session activities can be used as components for youth group meetings, religion classes, retreats, days of recollection, peer ministry meetings, small faith community gatherings, and so forth. Used in any of these ways, *Developing Faith* contributes to and is indeed a foundation for an expansive and engaging faith development program for youth.

A Model for Faith Development

Faith is fundamentally God's gift. It is God's personal offer of love and grace to each of us individually and to the community of believers we call church. Faith is also a human act. It is the response of trust, commitment, and submission that we make to God, both as individuals and as community.

The *Developing Faith* series is designed to help adolescent Christians develop the seeds of faith that were given to them at baptism. The *Rite of Baptism for Children* states that children who have been baptized as infants are to be brought up in such a way that they will gradually come to "accept for themselves" the faith in which they have been baptized (*RBC* 3).

Coming to accept the faith includes three distinct but interrelated processes: developing one's individual relationship with God, developing one's sense of belonging in a Christian community, and developing one's understanding of and allegiance to the institutional church. The *Developing Faith* series assists you, in your catechetical role, to help the adolescents in your charge focus on each of these processes.

First, the series is designed to help young Christians to be aware of and responsive to the presence of God in their daily lives. It contains a variety of prayer and reflection exercises that guide the participants to grow in their understanding of the mysterious relationship between themselves and God, and to deepen their personal commitment to developing that relationship.

Second, the series is designed to help the participating group—adults and youth—to interact as a faith community where Christian values are shared and deepened. It helps the youth to appropriate the value system that guides the daily lives of the Christian community. It calls them to direct their lives according to the meaning system of a living community whose members' lives reflect the presence of Jesus. It invites them to accept for themselves the gift of living faith that resides in the Christian community.

And finally, the series is designed to help the adolescent participants choose to be active members of the institutional church with all that such membership implies. It helps them to understand and value the systems of rituals, writings, teachings, and moral directives that have been preserved and handed on through the church. It shows how the sacraments, creeds, and doctrines of the church help both the individual and the community to own, express, and deepen the gift of faith.

About the *Developing Faith* Series

A mini-course consists of eight two to two-and-one-half hour catechetical sessions on a variety of appropriate subjects for high-school religious education. The series is for religious education directors, youth ministers, catechists, teachers, and teenagers who are involved in a faith development program (i.e., youth ministry, religion class). The series is also for other adults from the local faith community who will join with the youth to provide a full experience of faith development.

Adult Participation

A mini-course can be conducted with any size group of teenagers, provided there is enough adult participation. An ideal size is thirty to forty teen participants,

The success of the faith development program is dependent on the participation of adults who take up various roles. Adult roles and their definitions are as follows:

Coordinator of the program

This person organizes the program and gets it started by contacting adult volunteers, inviting the teens, setting the calendar, arranging for the meeting place, and holding initial organizational meetings. (This person may be the DRE, youth minister, theology department chairperson, retreat director, or any other person charged with setting up a faith development program for teens.)

Director(s) of the session

This person studies the *Director's Manual*, prepares and teaches the sessions, directs the other activities, and gathers the materials needed for each session. It is helpful if the director has teaching experience.

Group moderators

Each moderator is assigned a group of about six to eight participants. This grouping—unlike the small discussion groups formed at each session—remains the same for the entire program. The moderators attend all the sessions if possible. They check the attendance of their groups, contact those who are absent or tardy, arrange for makeup work, check and record homework assignments and teen-mentor meeting summaries, arrange and moderate service opportunities, etc.

Mentors

Ideally, these are adults who are paired one-on-one with the teens. They attend some of the sessions and meet with the teens between sessions. In the individual teen-mentor meetings, the mentors dialogue with teens about issues raised in a session, work on activities together, socialize, have fun, and offer many other kinds of support. The mentors form a strong link between the teens and the adult faith community. More information on the spiritual mentoring concept is offered on pages 10-11 and in the *Mentor Handbook*.

Parents, relatives, adult friends, and neighbors of the teen participants

These persons are invited to attend as many sessions as possible. The ideal is to have at least one group moderator and one visiting adult present in each discussion group.

Total parish community

There are many ways to involve the entire parish community in a faith development program. Besides the roles mentioned above, parishioners may also serve as prayer partners (adults who pray for individual teens). Teens should be invited to attend and participate in functions of parish organizations. Occasional Sunday liturgies should be geared to teenage tastes and interests (with teens involved in the planning and various liturgical roles). Announcements at weekly liturgies should mention current courses and events being offered in the program.

Program Features

The *Developing Faith* series consists of the following components:
- *Director's Manual*
- *Participant Book*
- *Mentor Handbook*

The *Director's Manual* presents very detailed lesson plans, including a script for the input section of the sessions and directions for conducting all activities. The *Director's Manual* also lists the objectives for each session, an overview of the session content, a time estimation of the session sections, suggestions for the physical setting, and a detailed list of needed materials. One copy of the *Director's Manual* is needed for each person who will help to direct the sessions.

The sessions combine various kinds of process activities: theological input, dialoguing, faith sharing, and fun. Hence, the *Participant Book* is not a typical "read-around-the-room" text. Rather, it includes stories, surveys, questions, exercises, and prayers that flow from the sessions themselves. It also includes occasional home assignments and directions for meetings between the teen and the mentor. You will need one copy of the *Participant Book* for each participant, session director, group moderator, and several extra copies for use by the adults who attend the individual sessions. The mentors may also want their own copies of the *Participant Book*.

The *Mentor Handbook* includes an overview of the spiritual mentoring component of the program and a list of qualifications and requirements for mentors. One copy of the *Mentor Handbook* is needed for each mentor. The program coordinator should also keep a copy.

Settings

The mini-course sessions use a variety of settings. In an ideal situation all of the following kinds of spaces would be available. Of course, you will have to adapt to the space you have available:

Large-group presentation space

An area where the entire group can be seated on beanbag chairs, floor cushions, or chairs close to the director and the board.

Discussion tables

A space where the participants can meet in groups of six to eight, preferably around square or round tables. Long narrow cafeteria tables do *not* work for discussion groups because they spread the group out too far. If small tables are not available, form discussion groups without tables.

Cozy corners

Comfortable spaces where each of the small groups can gather. These spaces are often in the corners of the main large group room. Couches, beanbags, or floor cushions are helpful.

Prayer space

A comfortable area, preferably carpeted, large enough so the group can sit on the floor in a circle. It may be possible to use the church sanctuary for this part of the activities.

"Alone" spots

A space large enough for the participants to spread out for quiet times of individual prayer and reflection (but within voice and eye range of the director). The church, gym, or cafeteria works for this. A supply of cushions or carpet pieces is helpful.

Especially for smaller groups, certain sessions or parts of sessions may be conducted in the homes of either the adults or participants.

Eight Two to Two-and-One-Half Hour Sessions

Each mini-course includes eight sessions. Each session is designed to be used in a period that lasts for two to two-and-one-half hours. The eight sessions function best as a complete course. Though each session is self-contained, one lesson draws from the others. Each session includes fun and community-building activities, solid catechetical input, discussion techniques that help the participants assimilate the material presented, and an individual or group prayer experience. It is *possible* to use each session separately or segments of the material in shortened sessions, but the eight-session, two to two-and-one-half hour package has been created as a distinct unit and will be most effective when used as a whole.

About This Mini-Course

Jesus, Should I Follow You? is a *core* subject mini-course in the area of Christology. While series' introductions of this kind generally offer an overall breakdown of the specific sessions of a course, the *Developing Faith* team of authors has chosen to place this background information in the **Overview** panels for each session to allow for easier access when a session is being prepared for and used.

Additionally, the *Developing Faith* team, understanding the variety of backgrounds, skills and experiences of adolescents, refrains from offering a specific age recommendation for this course. This is a course that is accessible to a wide-range of adolescents in many different settings. Only you can determine if this mini-course is right for the adolescents in your group

Mentor Concept

A distinct part of the *Developing Faith* series is the inclusion of the mentor component. In sum, a mentor is an adult from the local parish community who functions as a spiritual companion, adviser, counselor, and trusted friend to one or more candidates. The mentoring component is a tangible way for the adult members of the faith community to assist in the faith development of its adolescent members.

The mentor functions in this role in a series of informal one-on-one meetings with a teenager who is enrolled in the program. A detailed explanation of the qualifications and requirements of the mentor's role is presented in the *Mentor Handbook*.

Implementing the Mentoring Component

The mentoring component in a faith development program is ongoing. Here are some initial steps for implementation:

1. **Recruitment of Mentors** Announce the Mentor Information Meeting well in advance through the usual parish channels. Ask the teens to invite adults they know to the meeting.

2. **Mentor Information Meeting** Those interested in being mentors (and parents) are oriented to the mentoring concept and requirements at a Mentor

Information Meeting. After the meeting those who are still interested are interviewed and registered. Generally, one Mentor Information Meeting is held at the beginning of each program year and, if the numbers warrant it, the meeting can be repeated for new potential mentors and parents at the beginning of each block of mini-courses. (The complete Mentor Information Meeting plan is on pages 20-27).

3. **Pairing Teens and Mentors** After the meeting, the program coordinator and adult leaders finalize the pairings of teens and adults. A formal introduction of teens, parents, and mentors is arranged. It is recommended that the introductions take place at an informal reception held about thirty minutes prior to the first session.

4. **Teen-Mentor Meetings** One teen-mentor meeting plan with directions for conducting a meeting is included for each group session in the *Participant Book*. You may ask the teens and mentors to meet individually once between each session or once between every two sessions.

Messages to Mentors

The program coordinator or session director can communicate invitations to mini-course sessions, reminders about dates of upcoming events, specific activity assignments, and the like by asking the participants to write the message in the space titled "Mentor Memo" on the teen-mentor meeting page in the *Participant Book*.

Home Assignments

Home assignments are occasionally called for. Directions for some home assignments are given at the end of several sessions. At the teen-mentor meetings, the mentors are asked to choose one of three activities for the teen to complete. The activity itself or a written summary of what was done is checked by the group moderators at the next session.

How to Use the *Developing Faith* Series in a Complete Faith Development Program

The *Developing Faith* mini-courses are designed to fit comfortably into many different programming models. There is much freedom to adapt the mini-courses to many time-frames, settings, and existing academic calendars, or to use the mini-courses in a way that best meets the needs of your course or program.

Listed below are some ways to get started, common programming models, suggestions for scheduling, and other implementation and application notes.

Getting Started

An advantage of the eight-session mini-course is that you are more likely to be able to find adults to serve as session directors and moderators because of the shortened time commitment. To prepare adults to use the *Developing Faith* series in your parish, the following steps are recommended for the program coordinator:

1. Gather a group of interested adults to serve as group moderators. You will need one adult for every six to eight teen participants. It's better to approach volunteers through a personal network of connections in the parish rather than through a soliciting announcement in the parish bulletin. It is helpful if some of the volunteers have had experience in teaching or working with teenagers, but all do not need this background. What *is* needed is a love for teens.

2. Set up an organizational meeting for the adults. Share a presentation of the entire program based on the material found in this manual. This will provide the flavor of the program as well as the rationale. Other things for the program coordinator to do at this organizational meeting:

    - Ask each person to become familiar with the *Developing Faith* components: the *Director's Manual, Participant Book* and *Mentor Handbook*. Recommend that all read the introductory material in the *Director's Manual* for a thorough grounding in the theory and methodology of the program. Also recommend that they pay special attention to the Eight Be-Attitudes for Session Directors and Dialogue: Why and How sections in the Appendix, pages 115-118.

    - Decide on the director(s) for each session. It's best that one person serve as director for all eight sessions, though it is possible for more than one person to share the role.

    - Finalize as many dates as possible on the faith development program calendar. It is recommended that you schedule the Mentor Information Meeting several weeks before Session 1 to allow time to organize the adult leaders after they have experienced the method of this program in action.

    - Schedule a second organizational meeting, preferably after the Mentor Information Meeting.

3. Meet at a second organizational meeting. At the second organizational meeting the program coordinator should give directions for planning the subsequent sessions and other events. An agenda would include these tasks:

    - Assign each teen to a group moderator, who will check attendance, homework, service projects, and so forth for his or her group.

    - Decide how you will involve parents, mentors, and the total parish in the individual sessions. One simple method of assuring ongoing adult participation at the sessions is to make a list assigning each teen specific dates on which to bring an adult.

    - Plan a system of record keeping. It is important to have an accurate record of attendance, assignments completed, requirements fulfilled, etc. Records should be kept by the group moderators and turned over to the director at the end of the course.

Schedule and Content

One workable model is based on an academic year beginning in October and running through May. The year is divided into three eight-week trimesters and two four-week inter-terms.

Ideally, five or six mini-courses are offered each *trimester*. Mini-courses meet once a week at a variety of times and places. Service, social, and worship events (many in conjunction with the mentoring component) also take place. A sacramental preparation program weaves through the entire academic year.

During the *interterms* special events like teen retreats, service programs or projects, prayer services, and full- or half-day workshops on topics like sexuality or drug abuse are held.

The month of *September* is a time for registration, orientation, and information meetings.

The *summer months* are reserved for social events (camp outs, beach trips, and the like) and parish service projects (i.e., setting up a vacation Bible school for younger children), planning meetings, and vacation.

Youth Council

A youth council of twelve to fourteen high-school students from the parish with representatives from each grade is established. This group may be targeted and selected from recommendations from parents, teachers, pastoral staff, and other parishioners. The youth council meets regularly and works directly with the program coordinator and assistants to implement and maintain a total faith development program. Some of its tasks may include:

- helping to determine mini-course offerings (especially electives);
- developing, conducting, analyzing, and acting on the mini-course evaluations;
- arranging networking efforts between youth-sponsored programs and other programs within and outside of the parish;
- staffing and assisting at registration, workshops, service events, and retreats;
- surveying youth needs and suggesting ways to meet them;
- arranging and helping with social events like dances, camp outs, lock-ins, sports nights, amusement park trips, etc.

Requirements for Teens

Each participant may be required to take one, two, or three mini-courses (according to grade or age level) and one or more elective mini-course of his or her choice per year.

*What is a **required** mini-course?* The definition of a required mini-course can be determined by the program coordinator, adult assistants, and the youth council. Choices should be made on content and age-appropriateness. The following are just some examples of what may be required mini-course topics:

Developing Faith 13

Jesus
Sacraments
Catholic Identity
Church History
Hebrew Scriptures
Christian Scriptures
Self-Esteem
Morality

*What is an **elective** mini-course?* Elective mini-courses may explore a more specialized subject related to faith. Elective mini-courses are often based on the area of expertise or interest of the session directors. The program coordinator, adult assistants, and youth councils can survey the teens and the entire parish community for ideas about possible elective mini-courses. The following are just some of the examples of elective mini-course titles:

Forgiveness as a Solution to Racism

Media Awareness

How Sports Parallel Religion

Prayer and Spirituality

Comparing World Religions

Each participant is also required to attend two half-day workshops or one full-day workshop, one liturgical or prayer experience, and complete one major service project per year.

Sacrament Preparation

Preparation for the sacrament of confirmation is a part of many high-school faith development programs. Confirmation preparation adapts well to this model. The *Confirming Faith* program (Ave Maria Press, 1995), for example, includes twelve sessions. In an academic year divided into trimesters, sessions 1-4 are held in the first trimester, sessions 5-8 in the second trimester, sessions 9-12 in the third trimester. The sessions meet every two weeks. The inter-terms are used for retreats and service projects or to make adjustments in the overall schedule, for example, due to receiving an earlier confirmation date from the diocesan office.

The trimester model also lends itself to scheduling a religious-literacy course for teens who have received little or no religious training. This course can be used as a "catch-up" or review course for teens interested in receiving one or more of the initiation sacraments.

Any baptized person has the right to be confirmed. However, in order to ensure the integrity of the sacrament and the faith community, it is recommended that some basic catechetical prerequisites are observed. Many parishes require a *minimum* of one year's participation in a catechetical program before a candidate can begin immediate preparation for reception of a sacrament.

Sample Calendar

Listed on the next three pages is a sample calendar of a faith development program based on the trimester model. This list of courses (designated on the calendar by "MC") and activities is not exhaustive. Generally, three of the course offerings per trimester are required courses. The required courses as well as the number and titles of the electives can vary from trimester to trimester.

Fall Trimester

August

SUNDAY	MONDAY	TUESDAY	WEDNESDAY	THURSDAY	FRIDAY	SATURDAY
	1	2	3	4	5	6
7	8	9	10	11	12	13
14	15	16	17	18	19	20
21	22	23	24	25	26	27
28	29	30	31			

- Aug 1–6: Install new youth council and meet in first of regular monthly meetings; plan fall trimester schedule
- Aug 8–13: Begin bulletin announcements for fall trimester
- Aug 15–20: Continue ongoing youth social activities (sports nights, field trips, movies, roundtables, etc.)
- Aug 22–27: Meet with fall trimester mini-course and session directors

September

SUNDAY	MONDAY	TUESDAY	WEDNESDAY	THURSDAY	FRIDAY	SATURDAY
				1	2	3
4	5	6	7	8	9	10
11	12	13	14	15	16	17
18	19	20	21	22	23	24
25	26	27	28	29	30	

- Sep 1–3: Continue announcements for fall trimester (including Mentor Information Meeting and sacramental preparation)
- Sep 5–10: Commission program directors and moderators at Catechetical Sunday liturgy
- Sep 12–17: Register fall trimester participants (including confirmation preparation candidates)
- Sep 19–24: Conduct orientation meetings (i.e., Confirmation Introductory Meeting and Mentor Information Meeting)
- Sep 26–30: Continue ongoing youth meetings and activities

October

SUNDAY	MONDAY	TUESDAY	WEDNESDAY	THURSDAY	FRIDAY	SATURDAY
						1
2 MC1 9:30 am / MC2 6:00 pm	3 Youth Council	4 Confirmation Session 6:30 pm	5 MC3 7:00pm	6 MC4 7:00 pm / MC5	7	8
9 MC1 9:30 am / MC2 6:00 pm / Rite of Welcome and Commitment	10 Open Gym	11	12 MC3 7:00pm	13 MC4 7:00 pm / MC5	14	15 Lock-in
16 Lock-in Cont. / MC1 9:30 am / MC2 6:00 pm	17 Movie Night	18 Confirmation Session 6:30 pm	19 MC3 7:00pm	20 MC4 7:00 pm / MC5	21	22
23 MC1 9:30 am / MC2 6:00 pm	24 Open Gym	25	26 MC3 7:00pm	27 MC4 7:00 pm / MC5	28	29
30 MC1 9:30 am / MC2 6:00 pm	31 Halloween Trick or Treating					

November

SUNDAY	MONDAY	TUESDAY	WEDNESDAY	THURSDAY	FRIDAY	SATURDAY
		1	2 MC3 7:00pm	3 MC4 7:00 pm / MC5	4	5
6 MC1 9:30 am / MC2 6:00 pm	7 Youth Council	8 Confirmation Session	9 MC3 7:00pm	10 MC4 7:00 pm / MC5	11	12
13 MC1 9:30 am / MC2 6:00 pm	14 Open Gym	15	16 MC3 7:00pm	17 MC4 7:00 pm / MC5	18	19 Hay Ride
20 MC1 9:30 am / MC2 6:00 pm	21 Movie Night	22 Confirmation Session	23 MC3 7:00pm	24 Thanksgiving Dinner for Homeless and Poor	25	26
27	28 Open Gym	29	30			

January

(Winter Trimester / Interterm)

SUNDAY	MONDAY	TUESDAY	WEDNESDAY	THURSDAY	FRIDAY	SATURDAY
1	2 Youth Council	3	4	5	6	7
8 MC1 6:00 am	9 Open Gym	10 Confirmation Session	11 MC2 7:00 pm MC3	12 MC4 7:00 pm	13 Horror Movie Lock-In	14 MC5 9:00 am
15 MC1 6:00 am	16 Movie Night	17	18 MC2 7:00 pm MC3	19 MC4 7:00 pm	20	21 MC5 9:00 am
22 MC1 6:00 am	23 Open Gym	24 Confirmation Session	25 MC2 7:00 pm MC3	26 MC4 7:00 pm	27	28 MC5 9:00 am
29 MC1 6:00 am	30 Pizza Bash	31				

← Registration for Winter Trimester →

March

(Interterm)

SUNDAY	MONDAY	TUESDAY	WEDNESDAY	THURSDAY	FRIDAY	SATURDAY
			1 MC2 7:00 pm MC3	2 MC4 7:00 pm	3	4 MC5 9:00 am
5	6 Youth Council	7	8 Seminar: The Passion of Jesus 6:00pm	9	10	11 Ski Trip
12 Ski Trip Cont.	13 Open Gym	14	15	16	17 Soup Supper Sponsor 6:00pm	18 Day Workshop: Drug Awareness 10:00am
19	20 Meeting for Next Year's Youth Council Candidates	21	22 Communal Reconciliation Service	23	24 Confirmation Retreat	25 Confirmation Retreat
26 Clothing Canned Food Drive Ends	27	28	29	30 Holy Thursday Mass of the Lord's Supper	31 Good Friday Living Stations of the Cross Presentation	

← Holy Week →

December

(Winter Trimester / Interterm)

SUNDAY	MONDAY	TUESDAY	WEDNESDAY	THURSDAY	FRIDAY	SATURDAY
				1 MC4 7:00 pm MC5	2	3
4 "Giving Tree" Service Project	5 Youth Council	6	7	8	9 Weekend Retreat	10 Weekend Retreat
11 "Giving Tree" Service Project Weekend Retreat	12 Open Gym	13 Infancy Narrative Seminar Part I 7:00pm	14	15 Infancy Narrative Seminar Part II 7:00pm	16	17 Christmas Dance
18 "Giving Tree" Service Project	19	20	21 Free Babysitting for Christmas Shoppers	22 Christmas Caroling	23	24 Youth Mass
25	26	27 Sexuality Seminar Part I 7:00pm	28	29 Sexuality Seminar Part II 7:00pm	30	31 New Years Eve Lock-In

February

(Winter Trimester)

SUNDAY	MONDAY	TUESDAY	WEDNESDAY	THURSDAY	FRIDAY	SATURDAY
			1 MC2 7:00 pm MC3	2 MC4 7:00 pm	3	4 MC5 9:00 am
5 MC1 6:00 am	6 Youth Council	7 Confirmation Session	8 MC2 7:00 pm MC3	9 MC4 7:00 pm	10	11 MC5 9:00 am Valentine's Day Progressive Dinner
12 MC1 6:00 am	13	14 Fat Tuesday Ice Cream Party	15 MC2 7:00 pm MC3 Ash Wednesday Service 5:00pm	16 MC4 7:00 pm	17	18 MC5 9:00 am
19 MC1 6:00 am	20	21 Confirmation Session	22 MC2 7:00 pm MC3	23 MC4 7:00 pm	24 Soup Supper Sponsor 6:00pm	25 MC5 9:00 am
26 MC1 6:00 am	27	28				

Spring Trimester

April

SUNDAY	MONDAY	TUESDAY	WEDNESDAY	THURSDAY	FRIDAY	SATURDAY
						1
2 Easter	3 Youth Council	4 Confirmation Session	5	6	7	8
9 Rite of Acceptance	10 Volleyball League	11 MC1 7:00pm MC2	12 MC3 6:00pm	13 MC4 7:00pm MC5	14	15 Amusement Park Trip
16	17 Trivial Pursuit Tournament	18 MC1 7:00pm MC2 Confirmation Session	19 MC3 6:00pm	20 MC4 7:00pm MC5	21	22
23	24 Volleyball League	25 MC1 7:00pm MC2	26 MC3 6:00pm	27 MC4 7:00pm MC5	28	29
30						

↓ Registration for Spring Trimester ↓

May

SUNDAY	MONDAY	TUESDAY	WEDNESDAY	THURSDAY	FRIDAY	SATURDAY
	1 Youth Council	2 MC1 7:00pm MC2 Confirmation Session	3 MC3 6:00pm	4 MC4 7:00pm MC5	5	6
7	8 Volleyball League	9 MC1 7:00pm MC2	10 MC3 6:00pm	11 MC4 7:00pm MC5 Ascension Day	12	13 Family Reconciliation Service
14 Mother's Day Buffet Youth Council Election	15 Movie Night	16 MC1 7:00pm MC2 Confirmation Session	17 MC3 6:00pm	18 MC4 7:00pm MC5	19 Confirmation Rehearsal	20 Sacrament of Confirmation
21 Youth Council Election Pentecost	22 Volleyball League	23 MC1 7:00pm MC2	24 MC3 6:00pm	25 MC4 7:00pm MC5	26 Christian Service Projects Due	27
28	29	30 MC1 7:00pm MC2	31 MC3 6:00pm			

↑ Campaigning for Youth Council ↑

June

SUNDAY	MONDAY	TUESDAY	WEDNESDAY	THURSDAY	FRIDAY	SATURDAY
				1	2	3
4	5	6	7	8	9	10
11	12	13	14	15	16	17
18	19	20	21	22	23	24
25	26	27	28	29	30	

- Last sessions of mini-courses
- After Confirmation session
- Sponsor Vacation Bible School for primary children
- Evaluate year's programs
- Continue regularly scheduled events (i.e., gym night, movie night, etc.)

July

SUNDAY	MONDAY	TUESDAY	WEDNESDAY	THURSDAY	FRIDAY	SATURDAY
						1
2	3	4	5	6	7	8
9	10	11	12	13	14	15
16	17	18	19	20	21	22
23	24	25	26	27	28	29
30	31					

- Last meeting of current Youth Council
- Catechetal training and enrichment
- Plan next academic year's mini-courses; search for volunteers
- Conduct major social and service events (i.e., camp outs, beach trips, Habitat for Humanity, etc.)

Using the *Developing Faith* Series in Other Models and Settings

Flexibility is a main feature of the *Developing Faith* series. Using an eight-session course is not limited to the trimester model. Here are brief descriptions of some other models:

Sixteen-week semester course in a parish faith development program.

Schedule one session every two weeks. Assign teen-mentor meetings in the alternate weeks.

Eight-week quarter course in a parish faith development program.

Schedule mini-courses similar to the trimester model. Eliminate the interterms. The academic calendar would include four quarters running from October through May.

Sixteen-week semester course in a school setting.

Eliminate the opening activity. In the first week, reserve one class period to do Part I of the session. In the second week, reserve a second class period to do Part II of the session. Continue over a sixteen-week semester. The process-style lesson can provide a break from more traditional teaching methods used during the rest of the week. The mini-course material can be used to supplement or enrich the rest of the school course.

Eight-week quarter course in a school setting.

Divide the mini-course session into three approximately fifty-minute sections. Use the sections on a Monday-Wednesday-Friday basis in class.

Mini-workshop or retreat.

The mini-course subject matters can be used as the main themes of a mini-workshop or retreat. The session plans can be abridged to fit the specific time frame.

Advance Preparation

Long-term planning is helpful for whatever programming model is chosen. All eight session plans should be previewed by the session director(s). Supply lists should be compiled, music and video ordered, settings arranged, and special preparations made prior to the start of the course.

Orientation Meeting

Mentor Information Meeting

Objectives

The purpose of the Mentor Information Meeting is to gather potential adults who are interested in the role of the mentor:

- to share with them the model of faith that is the basis of this faith development program;
- to present the qualifications and requirements of the mentoring role;
- to conduct one-on-one interviews with the potential mentors and mutually decide if the role of mentor is for them.

Overview

This meeting is designed to allow interested adults a taste of the process-style the teens will experience in each mini-course session. A faith-sharing activity, a large group presentation, and a prayer experience are the main parts of the meeting. The adults are introduced to the faith model at the core of this series: the three aspects of faith (personal, communal, and institutional) and how the faith reality is nourished by caring members of the faith community throughout the long journey of life. This meeting also explains more about what being a mentor for a teen entails. Those who are sufficiently interested in becoming mentors are then individually interviewed to mutually determine whether or not this role is for them. The interviewers and program coordinator gather after the interviews to share their information, determine a roster of mentors, and match unattached teens with adults on the list.

Session Outline

I. Who Are Mentors? (about 40 minutes)
II. Model of Faith (about 15 minutes)
III. Prayer Experience (about 15 minutes)
IV. Break (about 5 minutes)
V. The Mentoring Component—More Information (about 15 minutes)
VI. Questions and Answers (about 10 minutes)
VII. Interviews (about 20 minutes)

Supplies

You will need the following supplies:
- name tags
- a schedule with times and dates of important events in the program
- newsprint (one large sheet for each table)
- markers (one set for each table)
- copies of the *Mentor Handbook*
- pencils
- recording of instrumental background music (optional)
- copies of Resource 1, the Mentor Interview and Registration Form
- a few copies of the *Participant Book* for each interview station

Special Preparations

At the end of the meeting, a time is reserved for those interested in being a mentor to be interviewed. Orient an interview team to (1) conduct interviews and (2) offer input into the pairing of teens with adult mentors. One interviewer (pastor, parents, pastoral staff) is needed to interview every four adults interested in being a mentor.

Setting

You will need the following areas for this meeting:
1. An area where the participants can meet around tables in groups of about eight.
2. An area where you can gather all the participants for the presentations. Arrange the chairs around a podium and chalkboard.
3. A large open area where everyone can gather in a circle for prayer.
4. An area for one-on-one interviews. A writing surface (either a table or clipboard) is needed for each interview area. There should be enough space between interview areas for privacy.
5. A hospitality area with coffee and refreshments.

I. Who Are Mentors?

(about 40 minutes)

Welcome

1. Moderators welcome the participants as they arrive, ask them to make their name tags, and distribute copies of the *Mentor Handbook*. The participants are directed to the small group tables. When everyone has arrived, formally welcome the group and thank them for coming. Present a talk based on the following material as it corresponds to pages 7–14 of the *Mentor Handbook*.

Definitions and Examples

2. Briefly overview the mentoring concept, either from the Greek legend or as the concept applies to your program. Concretize the examples of mentors listed on pages 7–8 by sharing stories (from your own experience or those of teens you have worked with) of mentors you know who are:

   Teachers
   Tell about a teacher who influenced you in your teen years or about a teen you know who was encouraged to develop his or her interests and talents at the direction of a teacher.

   Coaches
   Under this category fall mentors who inspire an appreciation of teamwork as individuals join together to work for a common goal. Tell about an athletic coach, drama teacher, band leader, or another person you know who has had great success working with teens.

   Older Relatives
   Good listening is an unappreciated yet vital skill. Many teens have adult relatives (other than mom or dad) who they can talk with about anything. Sometimes neighbors, family friends, and others in the parish family fill this role. Share a story you know about an adult who provides a nonjudgmental ear to a teen and the positive effect the person has had on the teen's life.

3. Briefly explain how the traditional role of a Christian sacramental sponsor is similar to that of a mentor's role (see *Mentor Handbook*, pages 9–11) and how a goal of this program is to return to the original concept of Christian sponsorship.

4. Overview how the teen-mentor relationship will function in the context of the faith development program (see *Mentor Handbook*, page 11) and the general characteristics of the teens who are enrolled in your program (see pages 11–13). Say:

   > Faith sharing is an essential part of this program, both in the class sessions and in the individual meetings between teens and mentors. The program is based on two fundamental principles of the *National Catechetical Directory:* (1) that total catechesis always includes sharing in the faith-life of a community; and (2) that the entire parish community is responsible for the catechesis of its members.

5. Point out the qualifications and requirements of a mentor in your program (see *Mentor Handbook*, pages 13–14).

Faith Sharing

6. Pass out a piece of newsprint and a set of markers to each table group. Take the participants through the reflection questions on page 9 of the *Mentor Handbook*. Say:

   > Who was a classroom teacher who was influential in your teen years? Write the person's name and a word to describe an important lesson he or she taught you. (Pause.)

> Who was an athletic coach, drama teacher, band leader, scout master (et al.) who encouraged you to develop and perfect an individual talent? Write his or her name and the name of the talent that was perfected. (Pause.)
>
> Who was an older relative or other adult you knew as a teen who you could count on for advice and to be a wise but non-judgmental friend? Write his or her name and a word to describe some wisdom that he or she imparted to you. (Pause.)
>
> Now please share with your group why your teacher was so influential. The person with the biggest watch can begin. Then go around the circle again and tell about how your talent was perfected with the help of a special coach. Finally share something of the wisdom you learned from an older relative or other adult when you were a teen. (Allow a few minutes for sharing, then continue.)
>
> You are no longer a teen-ager. You are an adult who has already—if you think about it—been a mentor for others. Now you are considering providing the same kind of support to a teen in this program. Write the names of three teens you have mentored and the particular role (teacher, coach, relative) you had next to each name.
>
> Tell your group about one of these experiences of mentoring. The person wearing the most blue can go first.

II. Model of Faith

(about 15 minutes)

Ask the participants to focus their attention on the chalkboard. Summarize the material covered to this point. Say:

> Besides being a teacher, coach, or good listener, a mentor is a **model** (write) of how a person of faith lives in today's world; a **friend** (write) who comes to know the teen and the teen's maturing faith; a **guide** (write) who is also a confidant and listener; a **learner** (write) who is also interested in his or her own growing faith; and a **spiritual companion** (write) who shares prayer time with the teen and helps the teen to understand and accept the gift of faith. In this program, the adult mentor helps the teen to grow in faith in each of three closely related but very different aspects. These aspects are represented by the diagram on page 15 of the *Mentor Handbook*.

(Draw the faith model on the board. If some of the group are familiar with the model from other presentations, ask them to explain the three aspects of faith represented by the diagram. If the diagram is new to the group, or if you want to expand on the participants' explanations, proceed with an explanation based on the text on pages 14-16 of the *Mentor Handbook* or on page 7 of this manual.)

Developing Faith

III. Prayer Experience

(about 15 minutes)

1. Ask the participants to form a circle in a large group meeting space. (It would be preferable for the participants to sit on chairs; however, if this is not possible sitting on a carpeted floor will do.) Place a lighted candle in the center of the circle. Have one of the adult moderators start the musical accompaniment (live or on tape). Darken the room. Then, lead a prayer based on the following script.

Prayer Script

2. To illustrate the role of mentor as one who shares prayer, let us offer our own prayers of petition and thankfulness.

   Recall the stick person in the center of the faith model diagram that represents our personally experienced faith. Our awareness of God is a personal gift, contingent upon awareness of self and of reality. If you had to choose a way you most often experience the presence of God, what would it be? Witnessing a beautiful sunset? In the midst of personal tragedy? When a particular song plays on the radio? When you are with someone you love? Take a moment and reflect on a way you experience God's presence. Then share your way with the person sitting next to you. (Allow time for the reflection and sharing, then continue.)

   The Christian community—recall the wavy line on the diagram—struggles to live faith day by day. Accepting the living faith of a Christian community is a process of absorbing the values and meanings which the group espouses. The more vibrant the faith of the community and the more it informs the actions and decisions of the members, the more readily its faith is accepted by children, youth, and all initiates. We pray for our local faith community at <u>name of parish</u> (mention a need of the parish-at-large; for example, "a room to store food and clothing for our social justice outreach" or "for a successful semester in our religious education program") and respond, "Lord, hear our prayer."

   (Offer the participants the opportunity to pray for a need of the parish community or to offer thanks for a grace received by the community. Allow time for these individual prayers, then continue.)

   Accepting the formal faith system of the church—the outside circle—means coming to understand the meaning of the symbols, rituals, doctrines, and laws in which the faith has been expressed. It is a process of learning to delve beneath these symbols to discover the deeper faith realities they represent. We pray for our universal church (mention a need; for example, "for the pope" or "for an increase of vocations to the priesthood or religious life . . .") and respond, "Lord, hear our prayer."

   (Offer the participants the opportunity to pray for a need of the universal church or to offer thanks for a grace present in the universal church. Allow time for these individual prayers, then continue.)

   God, we your people offer these prayers from our heart.

> We ask that you remember the adults who have come here tonight.
>
> Inspire them in the task of modeling their faith to others.
>
> Help them to serve the role of mentor well.
>
> We pray also for the youth in our faith development program and for their families.
>
> We pray in Jesus' name.
>
> Amen.

IV. Break

(about 5 minutes)

Take a five-minute break. Have the group stretch and move the chairs (if necessary) back to their positions for a large group presentation.

V. The Mentoring Component— More Information

(about 15 minutes)

1. Ask the group to bring their *Mentor Handbook* to the large group meeting area. Pass out copies of the faith development program schedule. When everyone is ready, continue an overview of the mentoring component based on the material in the *Mentor Handbook*. Add explanation as needed for each of the points that follow.

The Teen-Mentor Meeting

2. Provide details about the date, time, and place of the formal introduction between the teen and mentor. Ideally, this formal introduction would take place at a reception prior to the first mini-course session (see page 30). At the time of the formal introduction, the teens and mentors exchange phone numbers and arrange the dates, times, and places of some or all of their meetings.

   Explain how often you will require the teens and mentors to meet.

   Point out that teen-mentor meeting plans are included with each session in the *Participant Book*. Go over the basic format as outlined on pages 17-19 of the *Mentor Handbook*.

Effective Communication

3. Read the foundational points of the dialogue process (see *Mentor Handbook*, pages 19-20). Expand on each point as necessary.

Mentoring More Than One Teen

4. Cover the section on pages 20-21 of the *Mentor Handbook* as it applies to your program.

Group Events

5. Explain that special events like attending sessions, social outings and retreats, working on service projects, and participating in liturgical events will be periodically required. If applicable, refer to any of these events already on the schedule. *Optional:* Arrange for an adult and teen from last year's mentor program to share their reflections, comments, and observations about the experience.

VI. Questions and Answers
(about 10 minutes)

Allow about ten minutes for questions from the participants.

VII. Interviews
(about 20 minutes)

1. While the group is still in the presentation area, briefly explain the purpose of the individual interviews. Say:

> If you remain interested in becoming a mentor for one or more of the youth in this program, we ask that you meet now with one of the adult team members at one of the interview stations. (Point them out.) We will be able to dialogue more about the qualifications and expectations of the mentoring program. We will answer any questions you still have. We will ask if you have been invited here by a specific teen or if you are open to being assigned to a teen who does not have a mentor. We will go over the first mentor meeting plan with you in more detail.
>
> While you are waiting for your interview, please enjoy coffee and refreshments. You may leave after your interview. Thank you for coming and we will see many of you again on _____ (mention the dates of the first mini-course sessions or other initial meeting dates you have scheduled for mentors, teens, and parents).

A host or hostess (maybe a teen from the Youth Council) can direct the participants to the refreshment table.

Interview Format

2. The interviewer is to conduct the interview in the following manner:

    Greet the person and ask him or her to fill in the first lines on the Mentor Interview and Registration Form (Resource 1). If applicable, also have the interviewee write the name of the teen who invited him or her to the meeting. Then, ask one or more of the following questions (jot notes on the registration form):

- How did you hear about this meeting?
- What interests you about being a mentor?
- What recent experiences relating to teens have you had?
- How do you feel you meet each qualification for the mentor role? (See page 13 of the *Mentor Handbook*.)
- How able are you to meet the requirements of the program? (See pages 13-14 of the *Mentor Handbook*.)

3. Refer to the *Participant Book*. Turn to pages 13-14, Teen-Mentor Meeting 1, and allow the interviewee the chance to examine its content. Ask if he or she has any questions. Explain as needed.

4. Remind him or her that at the end of each teen-mentor meeting the mentor is to sign and date the meeting verification section included for each session in the *Participant Book*.

5. Conclude the interview. Say:

> You will be contacted by phone with further instructions and information. Thank you very much.

After the Meeting

6. The members of the interview team turn in their copies of the Mentor Interview and Registration Form. Discuss specific comments.

7. Work together to pair teens and mentors.

8. Contact the mentors by telephone and/or mail about the first mini-course session (or other formal meeting date and time).

9. Call any adults you have not chosen to be mentors, for whatever reason. Thank them for their interest. Tell them their names will be kept on file.

Group Sessions

Jesus, Should I Follow You?

session One

Objectives

The purpose of this session is to help the participants:
- consider what might be gained from following Jesus;
- identify the difference Jesus can make in a person's life;
- begin seriously to consider their own readiness to respond to the invitation to follow Jesus.

Overview

How different is your relationship with Jesus now from the time you made your first communion? What difference would it make to your life had Jesus never been born? How will your life be different or any better if you choose to make a commitment to really follow Jesus? These are some of the questions the teens will explore in this session. In the Opening Activity, the participants play a version of the television game *The Price Is Right* to determine some of what they know about Jesus. The point is made that following Jesus is much different than a game of chance. Following Jesus requires making a daily decision to remain committed to him and his teachings. In Part I, the participants reflect on the difference Jesus has made in their own lives up until this point and ways that he can have even more of a positive effect in the future. Part II is a scripture-based activity in which the participants work in small groups to come up with an ad campaign to encourage others to follow Jesus.

Mentor Component

It is recommended that you invite the mentors, teens, and parents to a brief hospitality reception about thirty minutes before the start of this session to provide an opportunity for formal introductions. Plan to invite the mentors and/or parents to stay for the first session (optional). Preview the Teen-Mentor Meeting 1 plan on pages 13-14 of the Participant Book.

Session Outline

Opening Activity: I'll Follow You If The Price Is Right (about 25 minutes)
Part I: What A Difference Jesus Makes! (about 45 minutes)
Break (about 10 minutes)
Part II: What's In It for Me? (about 45 minutes)
Prayer Experience: I Will Follow You (about 15 minutes)
Feedback and Conclusion (about 10 minutes)

Supplies

For this session you will need:
- name tags for the entire group
- eleven larger name tags for the Prayer Experience readers
- (optional) CD player and recording of "I Will Follow You" from the film *Sister Act*
- first communion photographs (two or three of each participant)
- feedback slips (a stack of 3" x 5" slips of paper)
- markers
- pens
- the following objects: a pair of men's sandals, a vase, a basket, a hammer, and index cards with a price estimation for each item (based on today's prices)
- three large poster boards
- 8 1/2" x 11" poster boards (one piece for every three or four participants)
- VCR and monitor
- video copy of *It's A Wonderful Life* (set at the point where Clarence the guardian angel grants George's wish that he was never born)
- copies of Resource 2, "Jesus Panel Preparation Sheet" (See Special Preparation, below)
- bibles
- eleven copies of Resource 3, " A Conversation with Jesus"
- a bible marked to the following passage: Mt 16:24-28
- army recruitment poster or ad depicting "opportunity for adventure"
- a candle

Special Preparations

1. Arrange for a panel of three to five teens (slightly older in age than the participants) who are capable of giving a brief witness talk on what difference Jesus makes in their lives. Give each of the panelists a copy of Resource 2, "Jesus Panel Preparation Sheet," page 125, to help them ready for their presentation.

2. You will need to prepare three large poster boards. On one side, number the posters 1, 2, and 3 in large print. On the other side write the following words:

Poster 1: Sorry, but like the rich man, you only get to go away sad.

Poster 2: Everlasting happiness as a true follower and disciple of Jesus.

Poster 3: You get to follow Jesus, but only until the going gets rough… then you flee.

Settings

You will need at least three areas for this session:
1. A large group area where you can gather the groups in a relaxed and informal atmosphere. There should be viewing access to a board or easel.
2. An area where the participants can meet around tables in groups of about four.
3. "Alone" spots—places where the participants can be at least six feet away from anyone else.
4. An area for the Prayer Experience. The floor of the church sanctuary often works well. If this area is impossible to use, arrange the large group area into a comfortable setting for prayer.

Opening Activity: I'll Follow You If The Price Is Right

(about 25 minutes)

Welcome

1. If possible, play "I Will Follow You" as the participants arrive. If they do not already have name tags on, ask them to prepare one as they arrive, put them on, and sit wherever they wish in the large group area. Begin with a formal welcome and (if necessary) a quick go-around on names. Introduce the opening activity. Say:

> We are about to begin the first of eight sessions on the topic of Jesus. I'd like to start by showing you photographs of some of our participants as they looked on their first communion day many years ago. I will not share these photos to embarrass or make fun of them, but to emphasize the point that the people here at this session are obviously not strangers to Jesus. To quote the words of St. Paul to Timothy: "From infancy you have known the sacred scriptures" (2 Tm 3:15). Similarly, you've heard about Jesus for years: pre-school, religious education class, Mass, grandma's stories, world religion class, confirmation preparation, and even television. So, you may be thinking, why are we here talking about Jesus again? Let me answer that question by asking another: How many of you feel you know everything there is to know about Jesus and are willing to leave behind everything to be his follower this very instant? (Pause to highlight the non-reaction!) So maybe it *is* worth it for us to spend some time thinking more about Jesus.

2. Pass out the first communion photos and allow a couple of minutes for them to be shared. Then, collect them and continue. Say:

> It's obvious that you are no longer in pre-school or first communion class. You are not the same person you were when you were three or seven or even twelve years old. Yet, how different is the way you imagine Jesus, the way you address Jesus, your relationship with Jesus between those times and now? It's possible that you may be walking around with some of the same "little kiddy" notions you had about Jesus way back when.
>
> In this session we are going to begin to consider some more challenging notions about what it means to know and follow Jesus. To start out we will consider why anyone would want to follow Jesus in the first place. We'll also ask, "What difference would it make to follow Jesus?" And, "Do I even know who Jesus is?" That sounds like some pretty heavy stuff to begin with right off the bat, so let's start by lightening up a bit. We're going to play a game called "I'll Follow You If The Price Is Right". If you've ever seen *The Price Is Right* T. V. show, then you'll know how to play. If not, you'll learn as we go. So let's begin. I need three players. Raise your hands! Show some enthusiasm!

Game

3. Call the names of three enthusiastic players (follow each name with a loud, "Come on down!") and have them line up in front of the whole group. Ask each contestant to state his or her name, age, and school. Then, explain the object of the game using these or similar words:

> I will show you an object. You will need to guess as close as possible the correct price of the object (based on what you think it would sell at today's prices). I have written down the correct price of the item on a card. When I show you the item, you will have ten seconds to write down on your card what you think the correct price is. The one closest to the correct price is the winner of that round and gets to move on and be eligible for the grand prize! Any questions?

4. Display the first object, a pair of sandals. Place your price card down in front of the sandals so no one can see it. Give the contestants a marker and a card. Say:

> Our first item is something from Jesus' very own collection: a pair of sandals he once wore on a trip from Nazareth to Jerusalem. I want you to guess the price of these sandals (what their suggested retail price would be today) and write it down on your card. Audience, you can help by shouting out suggested prices. Contestants, you have ten seconds to record a guess.

5. One by one, invite the contestants to reveal their cards with their price guesses. Then turn over the card with the price you marked on it to determine the winner (the contestant who came the closest). Send them all back to their places but tell the winner you'll call him or her back for round two. Repeat the process two more times for round one. The other two items are:
    - a hammer from Joseph's carpenter shop
    - a vase from the Upper Room (site of the Last Supper)

When you've completed round one, call back the three winners to play round two. Play the same as before, this time using as your object the basket used by the boy who brought Jesus five loaves and two fish. The winner of this round gets to go to the final round for a chance to win the grand prize.

6. Display three large poster boards, numbered 1, 2, and 3 on the sides where all can see. On the concealed side, the following words should be written:

   Poster 1: Sorry, but like the rich young man, you only get to go away sad.
   Poster 2: Everlasting happiness as a true follower and disciple of Jesus.
   Poster 3: You get to follow Jesus, but only until the going gets rough . . . then you flee.

   Say:

   > For the final round, you have the opportunity to win the ultimate grand prize which is behind one of the "doors" you see displayed here. (The poster boards may be laid against a wall or against a low table.) Behind one of these doors is "Everlasting happiness as a true follower of Jesus." Good luck. You may select your door.

7. After the selection is made, reveal the doors not selected first, followed by the one selected. Ask the "audience" to give all the contestants a round of applause. Conclude the game. Say:

   > It might be fun if knowing and following Jesus was like playing a game of chance and that you could win by making a lucky pick. It would also be a pretty reckless way of doing something that holds the key to life or death. Following Jesus is not a game. It has nothing to do with luck and the choice itself is more difficult than it is easy. Following Jesus is a choice that requires thought and consideration. You are here because you are capable of doing that kind of thinking and considering. I invite you to devote your full attention to Jesus' personal invitation to be his follower. Don't leave your decision to chance or luck. Consider it carefully.

Part I: What A Difference Jesus Makes!

(about 45 minutes)

1. Assemble the group near the television monitor and the board. (The *It's A Wonderful Life* video should be cued to the preset place. Begin by saying:

   > When you look at the title of this session, "Jesus, Should I Follow You?" (refer to page 7 in the Participant Book) does another question come to mind? Like, "Why should I follow you?" Or, "What difference does it make if I follow you?" These are important questions to consider. (Point out the other questions on page 8.) Before you think about whether or not you are ready to be a follower of Jesus, you need to take some time to look at what difference it will or could make to your life. *What difference does Jesus make at all?*
   >
   > In the Christmas time movie, *It's A Wonderful Life*, George Bailey wishes he had never been born. His wish is granted and his guardian angel Clarence shows him what the world would have been like if he had never been born.

Video Presentation

2. Show the segment of *It's A Wonderful Life* from when Clarence grants George's wish until George runs back to the bridge pleading to get his life back (about twenty minutes).
   Optional: If you are not able to show the video, paraphrase the plot as well as you can or ask the students to construct several scenarios explaining how the world would be different had they not been born.

3. After showing the video segment, ask the participants to share several of the ways that the lives of the characters in the story would have been different had George never been born. Briefly list some of the ways on the board. Then, continue. Say:

   > The message of the movie is that every person makes an impact on the world—especially on people in close proximity to them. Thinking again about Jesus, it would be safe to say that Jesus has made an impact on the world. Even those who do not believe in Jesus as the Messiah, God's only son, the second person of the Trinity, find it hard not to include him on a list as one of the most influential figures of all history. Let's imagine for a moment that Jesus had never been born. Christmas never happened. No shepherds. No manger. No stable. No animals. No wise men. How would the world be different had Jesus never been born? Take a moment to think about some ways.

4. Allow some time for quiet thinking. Then ask the participants to share some of the ways. Make a new column on the board and list some of their ideas. After exhausting the list, tell the participants you would like them to personalize their responses a little bit more. Say:

   > Let's ask ourselves: "How would my life be different if Jesus had never been born?" Because it is so personal, you may find it difficult to put your responses into words. For that reason, I would like you to do an activity in your Participant Book.

Activity

5. Tell the participants to turn to "If Jesus Had Never Been Born," page 9 in their books. Explain that they are to read the directions and mark both sections. Ask them to take their books and a pencil to an "alone" spot and begin.

6. After about five minutes, tell the group to form triads with the two closest people. Ask them to share one or two reasons about why they checked the responses they did.

7. Call on one person from each triad (the person wearing the most blue) to report on one significant thing that was shared in their group about how an individual's life would be different had Jesus not been born. Briefly summarize in a third column on the board.

Summary

8. Say:

> For some people, if Jesus had never been born, it would be like ripping away the most important part of their lives. Other people may feel somewhat frustrated or embarrassed to realize that Jesus doesn't play such a big part in their lives after all. If that is the case for you, don't feel bad. It only means that you have yet to realize the full impact that Jesus can make on your life. But the fact that you are here, enrolled in a mini-course on Jesus, indicates that you are willing to give your relationship with Jesus more of a chance. Pray for yourself as you begin. Pray for guidance, patience, and determination. Hang in there! Jesus is inviting you to follow him. He can make a big difference in your life.

Break

(about 10 minutes)

Allow a ten-minute break. Display the first communion photos. (The participants might want to play a "guess who" game to identify the people in the photos.) Ask them to assemble in the large group area. (During the break welcome the panel of teens you have invited for the panel presentation.)

Part II: What's In It for Me?

(about 45 minutes)

1. Recap the Part I material as a lead-in to the next lesson. Say:

> To some degree great or small you have to admit the impact Jesus has had on your life and those around you. Still, you have heard many people (parents, teachers, priests) speak about the importance of basing an entire life around Jesus and you may be wondering why. In this lesson, we will look at some answers to the question "What's in it for me if I follow Jesus?"

Panel Presentation

2. Ask the panel of three to five teens to take their places. (You may wish to set chairs in front of the group or just have the teens join in various places in the group's configuration.) As they take their places, introduce them and the activity. Say:

> I've invited some teens who are just a little older than you to spend a few minutes sharing with us how they feel Jesus has made a difference in their lives in real, everyday, practical ways. As they share with you, make mental notes of some key words and phrases used by the panelists to describe the real and practical ways they feel their lives have been impacted by Jesus.

3. Ask the panelists to introduce themselves. Direct the panel discussion using the questions on Resource 2, "Jesus Panel Preparation Sheet," page 125. Allow about ten to fifteen minutes total for the panel to share.

4. Reserve a few minutes for the panelists to take questions and hear comments from the participants. Thank the panelists and invite them to stay for the rest of the session (optional).

Group Project

5. If you have been able to get an armed forces recruitment poster display it now. Point out that any group that seeks your membership (colleges, places of employment, teams, etc.) attempts to answer the question "What's in it for me?" for prospective members. Count-off the participants into groups of four or five. Then introduce the project. Say:

> We've listened to some teenage panelists tell us from their own experience what they "get" out of following Jesus. I asked you to make some mental notes while they were talking so that you could use them in a project. With your group, I want you to imagine that you have been given the responsibility of creating a recruitment poster for following Jesus. Your ad or campaign must be targeted at your own age group and it must be based on the kinds of things that were just shared with you by our panelists. In other words, don't make up a bunch of flowery and poetic promises (as nice as they may be) that you yourselves would never buy. Make it real. Make it something that will answer the question, "What's in it for me?"

6. Distribute the smaller poster boards and markers to each group. Instruct the groups to use the "Poster Think Sheet" on page 10 of the Participant Book to help them in the preparation process. Allow twenty minutes for the entire project. *Optional:* The groups may be allowed to develop a television commercial in skit form if they prefer.

7. Ask a group member (the person wearing the most jewelry) to share and report on the finished project. Display the posters in the room for the remainder of the session. Say:

> Now, if you need a good reason for following Jesus, just look around and read them!

Scripture Activity

8. Have the participants remain in their small groups. Call for runners to bring bibles (one for each person) back to their areas. Then, say:

> It's one thing to have an attractive advertising campaign, but ultimately it comes down to whether or not you are ready as an individual to respond. You may agree that the army or navy has an effective ad campaign, but if you are not ready to make a commitment (and all the sacrifices that go with it) to belong, it really doesn't mean a thing. Likewise, Jesus may offer us very attractive possibilities for our lives (not the least of these being eternal life), but if we are not ready to respond it won't make any difference.

Jesus, Should I Follow You?

9. Ask the participants to turn to "Finding Myself in Scripture," page 11 in their books. Explain that there are many different ways to respond to the challenge of following Jesus as evidenced by the way several disciples listed in the New Testament chose to follow. Make sure the participants understand the directions for the activity. Ask them to work alone. (You may need to help some individuals find the scripture passages.)
10. After about ten minutes, ask the participants to share their answers to the summary question with their small groups. (As the discussions are taking place, move through the room and select ten people for the reader parts in the upcoming Prayer Experience. You take the part of Jesus. Give them each a large or prominent name tag on which they can write their character's name from Resource 3. Ask them to put them on as the prayer begins.)

Prayer Experience: I Will Follow You

(about 15 minutes)

1. Ask the participants to return to the area you have designated for the Prayer Experience and arrange themselves in a circle. Distribute copies of Resource 3, "A Conversation with Jesus" to each person. Place the pair of sandals (from The Price Is Right game) in the center of the group along with a candle.
2. Dim the lights. Light the candle. Ask the participants to quiet themselves and ready their hearts for prayer. Say:

   > We began this session with a game and we used these sandals as a prop, pretending that they once belonged to Jesus. Since that time, we've covered quite a bit of ground. We can be sure of two things:
   >
   > - Jesus is calling us to follow him . . . and
   > - this is no game!
   >
   > Sandals are what Jesus wore in his time as he traveled from place to place. They are symbolic of his journey and so we keep them in our midst as a reminder of Jesus' invitation to each of us to walk the journey with him.
   >
   > We are all at different places when it comes to our readiness to respond. During this prayer, let us listen to the words that Jesus speaks to us. Let us place ourselves in a spirit of quiet and prayerfulness and pray that the Holy Spirit will open our minds and hearts to the word of God. (Pause.)

3. Reverently open the bible to Matthew 16:24-28. Read the passage (the doctrine of the cross) to the group.
4. Continue with Resource 3, "A Conversation with Jesus." Say:

   > Listen to this conversation with Jesus. The readers will express the words and feelings of some of the scripture characters we've read about. The words I respond with are the words of Jesus. Listen to what Jesus has to say to you.

5. To conclude, have everyone join hands and recite an Our Father. Play "I Will Follow You" from *Sister Act* (optional).

Feedback and Conclusion

(about 10 minutes)

1. Return to the small groups. Give each table a stack of feedback slips. Write the following sentence starters on the board:

    Something about the session I liked (or didn't like) was . . .

    The most important thing I learned was . . .

    One thing I would like to learn (or do) during this course is . . .

2. Instruct each person to complete at least one of the sentences. Encourage the participants to sign each paper, but tell them they do not have to.

3. Assign a group moderator to one or more of the small groups already formed. Tell the participants that they are to check-in with their moderator before each session and that their moderator will check assignments, monitor projects, and be available to answer any questions they might have.

Mentor Meeting Reminder

4. At this first session, it's important to clarify the teen-mentor meeting assignment. Remind the participants to bring their books to their meeting, to complete the teen-mentor meeting summary (page 14 of the Participant Book), and have the page signed by their mentor and returned by the group session you specify.

5. Collect the feedback slips and use them to help you evaluate the session. Dismiss the group on time.

Jesus, Can I Get to Know You Better?

session Two

Objectives

The purpose of this session is to help the participants:
- identify strategies they use for making new friends and getting to know people better;
- deepen their relationship with Jesus by applying the skills they have learned;
- become more familiar with some basic information regarding Jesus' life, circle of friends, and surrounding culture that can help them to know him better.

Overview

This session is a basic introduction to the life, times, and world of Jesus. The focus is to encourage and challenge the teens to get to know Jesus better as a way to develop a more personal relationship with him. A strategy to accomplish this is to relate how the participants establish relationships and make friends in their daily lives to how they can do the same with Jesus. A prayer experience provides an introduction to Jesus' call to friendship. A scripture activity helps the participants delve more deeply into the geographical, cultural, social, and religious atmosphere of Jesus' time on earth. The teens will also gain some sense of how, why, and when the gospels were recorded.

Session Two

Mentor Component
Preview Teen-Mentor Meeting 2 on pages 25-26 of the Participant Book.

Session Outline
Opening Activity: "Getting to Know (More About) You" (about 30 minutes)
Part I: Strategies for Making Friends (about 30 minutes)
Prayer Experience: Jesus Allow Me to Introduce Myself (about 15 minutes)
Break (about 5 minutes)
Part II: Getting to Know Jesus Better (about 60 minutes)
Feedback and Conclusion (about 10 minutes)

Supplies
For this session you will need:
- name tags
- markers
- pens
- a large picture of Jesus covered by a question mark
- a poster with the phrases "Nice to meet you!" and "Come, follow me!" printed large enough for all to see
- a candle
- a bible marked to the following passages: Jn 1:35-39; Phil 2:1-11; 1 Cor 13:8-13; Jn 15:9-17
- bibles (New Testament) for each participant
- masking tape
- copies of Resource 4, "Jesus, Allow Me to Introduce Myself," page 127
- tape or CD player
- recording of the Beatles' "Twist and Shout" or "She Loves You" or another of their well-known songs
- slips of paper with one biblical name written on each
- (optional) *The Compleat Beatles* video
- (optional) VCR and monitor

Special Preparation
Cover part of the picture of Jesus with a question mark. This can be done using masking tape to form a question mark on the picture or by drawing a question mark on a piece of paper and taping it to the drawing.

Settings
You will need the following areas for this session:
1. A large group area where you can gather the groups in a relaxed and informal atmosphere. There should be viewing access to a chalkboard or easel.
2. An area where the participants can meet around tables.

3. "Alone" spots—places where the participants can be at least six feet away from anyone else.
4. An area for the Prayer Experience (optional). The floor of the church sanctuary often works well. If this area is impossible to use, arrange the large group area into a comfortable setting for prayer.

Opening Activity: "Getting to Know (More About) You"

(about 30 minutes)

1. As the participants arrive, have the group moderators positioned at tables to take attendance and check their Teen-Mentor Meeting 1 summary and mentor's verification signature. During the arrival time, choose four teens to do the scripture readings for the Prayer Experience. Allow them a chance to preview the passages they will be reading.
2. After they have checked in, ask the participants to sit wherever they choose in the large group meeting area. They will most likely sit with their friends.
3. Ask the group moderators to distribute name tags and pens. Tell the participants not to write anything on the name tags until instructed. Have the group open their Participant Book to page 16, "Jesus' Family Tree." Then, say:

> In this session we are going to try to get to know Jesus better. To start, let's look at Jesus' ancestral roots—his family tree. As I call out a name on the list, a moderator will tap someone on the shoulder. If they tap you, write the name that was just called on your name tag. This is your biblical name. Then, under your biblical name, write your first name in parentheses. When you've done that put your name tag on.

4. Make sure two group moderators are positioned on opposite sides of the room. Begin slowly calling out the biblical names, alternating back and forth between columns and between the two adults assigning the names so that the partners are on opposite sides of the room. Do this until everyone in the group has been assigned a biblical name. (This will work for up to forty participants.) Don't worry about not reading all the names if you have fewer than forty participants.
5. When everyone has their name tag completed and on, say:

> Now, you must find the person in this room whose name appears next to yours on the Family Tree sheet in your Participant Book. Move around the room until you find your partner. Introduce yourself by your biblical name. Then sit together for the next activity.

Activity

6. After everyone is in place (the large group area works well for this activity providing there is enough space between one pair and another), ask the participants to open their books to page 17, "Getting to Know (More About) You." Say:

> In order to get to know Jesus better, let's polish up on some social skills with each other. Each person will have seven minutes to interview your partner using the questions on page 17-18. Record the information from your interview in the spaces provided. Be prepared to share what you think is the most interesting thing you learned about your partner with the entire group. After exactly seven minutes I will call time and you'll switch roles (if you haven't already done so). Ready, begin.

7. Six minutes into the interview, call for everyone to wrap up. At seven minutes, call time and ask the group to switch roles. Use the same procedure as before. When both sets of interviews are finished have the participants sit in a circle next to their partners. When the group is positioned, say:

> You will each introduce your partner to the group by their biblical name and their real name. When it's your turn, stand up and say, "This is Obed, also known as Melissa." Pronounce the biblical names the best you can. Then tell what you consider to be the most interesting thing you learned about your partner in the interview. The real Obed (or whatever name you choose) will go first. After Obed's group we'll move in a clockwise direction around the circle.

8. Continue the activity until everyone has been introduced. Then gather the group close to you. Make sure they are in a place where they can see the picture of Jesus with the question mark overlaid on his face.

Part I: Strategies for Making Friends

(about 30 minutes)

1. Point out the picture of Jesus with the question mark covering his face. Say:

> So this is the person we're trying to get to know better. Our relationship with Jesus—where it's been, what it is now, and where it's going—might be a big question mark for us. The only way for us to remove the question mark is to get to know Jesus better. To get to know Jesus better, let's step back for a few minutes and ask ourselves just how we go about getting to know anyone better, how we go about making friends. For example, think about when you first started high school and how you went about making new friends then.

Activity

2. Ask the participants to take their books and pens and move to an "alone" spot in the large group area. Say:

> To help you remember what it was like at the beginning of high school, turn to page 19 in your book. Read the essay, "Getting to Know (All About) You." Then write your responses to numbers 1-3 on the "Making Friends Worksheet," page 21.

Panel Report

3. After about eight minutes, have the group gather near you. Call out five names at random (use their biblical names from Jesus' family tree) and ask them to come forward and face the group. (You may want to have them sit in five chairs facing the group.) Conduct a discussion with the panelists based on their responses to question 2 on the "Making Friends Worksheet." Ask, "What appealed to you most about this friend?" Allow each panelist the chance to share all the things he or she checked. When the panel is finished sharing, take a show of hands to poll the entire group on the various responses to question 2. Dismiss the panel and call five more participants to take their places.

4. Ask the new panelists to relate what strategies they employed in getting to know this friend better (question 3). After they all have shared, poll the entire group to highlight the most common strategies. Dismiss the five panelists.

5. Have the participants answer questions 4 and 5 on the worksheet. When completed, ask them to pair up once again with their biblical partner and share their responses to those two questions. Allow about six to eight minutes.

6. As a way to sum up, poll the entire group on question 5. Write some of the most common responses on the board. Ask several of the participants to expand on these suggestions and how they might be applied to getting to know Jesus better. Leave the list on the board. Tell the participants to keep their pens with them.

Prayer Experience: Jesus, Allow Me to Introduce Myself

(about 15 minutes)

1. Place the poster with the words "Nice to meet you!" and "Come, follow me!" where all can see. Gather the group near the poster and the picture of Jesus with his face covered by a question mark. Ask them to prepare themselves in mind and attitude for prayer.

2. When the group has quieted, invite one participant to come forward and remove the question mark from Jesus' face. Then, lead a prayer experience based on the following script:

Prayer Script

3. We've spent some time looking at how we make friends, what attracts us to Jesus, and what strategies we can use to get to know Jesus better. Well, making friends goes both ways. Jesus himself is willing to meet us more than half-way when we desire to be his friend. In order for Jesus to do this, however, we have to reveal some of ourselves to him. We have to allow Jesus into our lives and let him get to know us better too.

   None of you are the same person you were when you were in third or fourth grade. If you ran into a teacher you had in those years you would have to re-introduce yourself because you look, act, and think differently now than you did then. The same is true in meeting up with Jesus again at your age. Since you are no longer a child, you need to establish a friendship that allows Jesus to see you as you are now: a teenager.

We're going to take this prayer time to re-introduce ourselves to Jesus and pray that our relationship with him will be strengthened. (Pause, darken the lights, and place a lighted candle in front of the picture of Jesus.) Let's focus our attention on Jesus as we continue our prayer. I invite you to listen to the following story:

There was once a handsome prince who had a crooked back. The crooked back kept him from being the kind of prince he was meant to be. One day, the prince's father, the king, commissioned the best sculptor in the kingdom to carve a statue of the prince. The finished art piece was masterful! It looked exactly like the prince in every detail but one: in the statue, the prince was portrayed with a straight back. The king placed the statue in the prince's private garden. When the prince first saw it, his heart beat faster. Months passed and the people began to say, "The prince's back doesn't seem as crooked as it was." When the prince heard these comments, his heart beat faster still. Now, the prince began to spend hours a day studying the statue and meditating on it until one day a remarkable thing happened. The prince found himself standing as straight as the statue.

(Pause in silence before continuing.)

Each of us is like the prince. We all have imperfections that keep us from being exactly who God intended us to be. However, when we look at Jesus our own heart skips a beat. We see someone standing spiritually straight and tall and we recognize ourselves in him. As a teenager, you may be more self-conscious about your imperfections (the way you look or act) than you ever were before. Jesus can help us to take a closer look at ourselves and see the goodness we have been gifted with by God. Listen to these words about Jesus, the one who stands straight and tall.

4. Place the bible with the marked scripture passages at a podium or table near the front of the group. Call readers 1-3 to the front and ask them to take turns reading their assigned passage:

    Reader 1   Jn 1:35-39 (Come, and you will see.)
    Reader 2   Phil 2:1-11 (Your attitude must be Christ's.)
    Reader 3   1 Cor 13:8-13 (When I was a child . . .)

Prayer Script (continued)

5. You are no longer children. You no longer think like children or act like children. You have put childish ways aside in so many of the things you do; in your schoolwork, your activities with friends, the responsibilities you have around your home. How well does Jesus know this new you? When is the last time you really told Jesus all the things going on in your life? Jesus invites you to share yourself with him. (Have the group moderators assist you in passing out Resource 4, "Jesus, Allow Me to Introduce Myself," page 127, to each participant.)

> I now invite you to re-introduce yourself to Jesus. Think about what you would say if you had a chance to meet Jesus face-to-face. What would you tell him about your life? What reasons would you offer him for wanting to be his friend? As you think about how you would answer these questions, fill in the sheet you've just been given. When you complete your sheet, come forward and take a piece of tape and tape it around the poster that shows Jesus' reply: "Nice to meet you!" and "Come, follow me." You may fold your sheet in half if you like. Please do this in a spirit of quiet and reflectiveness. Return to your place when you have finished.

6. Put on a recording of reflective background music and tell the participants to begin to follow the directions you just gave them. Move about (with the group moderators) to help those who seem to be having trouble and to help maintain the quiet. When everyone has posted their sheet, say:

> You have re-introduced yourself to Jesus and asked him if you can follow. Let's conclude our prayer by listening to his words to us.

7. Call on the assigned reader to read the following passage:
   Reader 4   Jn 15: 9-17 (I call you friends. . .)

Conclude by inviting anyone who wishes to do so to share anything they wrote or found meaningful in this activity.

Break

(about 5 minutes)

Allow a brief time for a stretch, drink of water, etc. Tell the participants to pick up a bible on the supply table and return to the large group area with their bible, book, and pen after the break.

Part II: Getting to Know Jesus Better

(about 60 minutes)

1. Gather the participants in the large group near the chalkboard or easel. Make sure the tape or CD player is cued with the Beatles' song you have chosen. Recap the session to this point and introduce this lesson. Say:

> We've looked at how we make friends, what attracts us to Jesus, and what strategies we can employ to get to know Jesus better. In order for us to move forward and learn more about Jesus' life and times, we have to get ourselves in a first-century state of mind. I'd like you to listen to this song. When it's over, we'll discuss how it can help us to get to know Jesus better. By the way, feel free to dance along.

2. Play a tape of an early and well-known Beatles' song such as "Twist and Shout" or "She Loves You." Encourage them to stand up and move to the music, '60s style. Since you told the group this song would help them get into the right frame of mind for getting to know Jesus, you'll probably get some puzzled groans.

However, when the song is over proceed with assurances that this song does give the right direction for the rest of the session.

Optional: You may want to show ten minutes of the video, *The Compleat Beatles* that depicts the hysteria that ensued when the Beatles arrived in the United States. This can be found in the music section of most video stores.

3. Begin the discussion by asking, "Does anyone know who that song was written and sung by?" When someone answers correctly, write **The Beatles** on the board and ask, "What are some things you know about the Beatles?" List everything the group can muster about the Beatles. (If it is not brought up, be sure to emphasize the hysteria that was caused by the Beatles' arrival in the U.S.) Ask: "Can anyone offer an explanation as to why there was so much excitement over the Beatles in the 1960s?" After listening to a few opinions, ask, "What would help us to understand 'Beatlemania' more fully?" Be sure to conclude that no understanding of the Beatles' phenomenon would be complete without:
   - listening to some of the Beatles' music (both original recordings and "cover versions");
   - watching some documentary that recorded the events of that time;
   - reading some news articles, features, and commentaries from periodicals of that time;
   - talking to someone who had experienced the events of Beatlemania firsthand.

4. Continue by saying:

   > I promised you that the song you heard would get you in the right frame of mind for getting to know Jesus better. Can anyone guess how this might be so? (If no one guesses, point out that just as we need to go back and understand the times and social climate of the world of the Beatles, we need to understand the times and world of Jesus in order to understand him better.)

5. Repeat the same type of brainstorming exercise for Jesus. Ask: "What are some things you know about Jesus?" List the responses on the board or easel. (The list doesn't have to be exhaustive; allow about ten minutes for the discussion.)

6. Make the connection between the two lists (Beatles and Jesus). Say:

   > We said that in order to fully understand the Beatles' experience, we had to delve into the music, do some research, and talk to some people who experienced Beatlemania firsthand. While it is impossible to talk with people who lived at the time of Jesus, we can talk to several people who claim to have a personal relationship with him today (though none of them ever knew the historical Jesus). We can also read the gospels to find out what Jesus did and said. We can research more about the time and place that Jesus lived from other historical sources. Let's begin the process with a scripture activity.

Scripture Activity

7. Ask the participants to form groups of four (two "biblical pairs" combine) and meet at a table with a bible, pen, and their book opened to page 22, "Looking for Clues." Go over the directions with the group. (The group moderators can assign

questions to each person and then ask them to share their answers.) Everyone in the group should write an answer for each question. Allow about fifteen minutes. Then, say:

> Each group should choose one or two of the findings they found most interesting and report on it to the large group. The person with the shortest biblical name in the group can be the reporter.

8. After all the groups have reported, continue the explanation. Say:

> We used the Beatles as an example of trying to understand an experience that happened long before we were around. The Beatles were from another country and arrived on the U.S. scene over thirty years ago. While their music is still played a great deal, it is difficult for a person your age to understand what all the excitement was thirty years ago. And, though Jesus is truly alive and present with us now, we still need to go back and understand what it was like when he walked the earth in order to know more about him. Jesus lived two thousand years ago in a culture much different from our own. He spoke a language (Aramaic) that none of us can understand. His first followers were fishermen, housewives, tax collectors, shepherds, and prostitutes. Let's look at some more specifics about the world in which Jesus lived and compare them with our own world.

Presentation

9. In order to illustrate, introduce a presentation called "Now and Then." Using the board or easel, list in one column what Jesus would encounter if he came into our world now, and in the other column what Jesus actually experienced then, two thousand years ago, in several categories. Invite the participants to provide answers to fill in each category of both the now and then columns. The following notes can help you to flesh out what is not mentioned. Be prepared to provide more input from your notes for the then column. Allow about twenty minutes.

Now and Then Notes

> ### *The World*
>
> **Now**
>
> **If Jesus came into our world now, he would encounter . . .**
> - **a civilization on the verge of the twenty-first century**
> - **a large nuclear arsenal in many nations**
> - **ethnic and social wars or fragile peace in many areas**
> - **a world in close communication due to advances in technology**
>
> **Then**
>
> **When Jesus came back then, he encountered . . .**
> - **a largely agrarian and even nomadic society**
> - **a great part of the world (and his entire world) ruled by the Romans**
> - **most communication handled orally**

The Topography

Now

If Jesus now came to our region, he would encounter . . .

- characterize your local region in terms of topography and environmental issues as well as by the ethnicity, economics, etc., of the area.

Then

When Jesus came back then, he encountered . . .

- an occupied land
- a native region that was 150 miles long and 50 to 60 miles wide
- a mix of mountains, deserts, valleys, fertile land, and rocky land
- bodies of water including the Sea of Galilee, Dead Sea, Red Sea, and Mediterranean Sea

The Politics

Now

If Jesus came now, he would encounter . . .

- capitalism
- democracy
- Republicans and Democrats
- a President, governors, mayors, etc.
- special interest groups (NRA, Civil Rights, conservatives, liberals, pro-choice, fundamentalists, etc.)

Then

When Jesus came back then, he encountered . . .

- the emperor of Rome
- tetrarchs, kings, procurators
- military occupation

The Religion

Now

If Jesus came now, he would encounter . . .

- a pluralistic society of many religions
- sixteen percent of the population claiming to be non-religious
- divisions among Christians
- the Lord's Supper celebrated world wide
- a successor of St. Peter serving as spiritual leader (the pope)
- great numbers of the Jewish population destroyed by the holocaust

Then

When Jesus came back then, he encountered . . .

- a Jewish society
- Pharisees (Jews who were religiously liberal with a pious commitment to the law; would not compromise with Roman rulers; received "bad press" in the Christian scriptures)
- Saduccees (priestly class of Jews who often compromised with Roman power; conservative in religion)
- Zealots (Jews who sought independence from Rome through military means)
- scribes (writers and interpreters of the Law)
- Sanhedrin (official Jewish governing body or "senate")
- High Priest (head of priestly class and president of the Sanhedrin)

The People/Friends

Now

If Jesus came now, he would encounter/befriend . . .

- people with AIDS
- homeless people
- prisoners
- oppressed ethnic, religious, and social groups
- unemployed

Then

When Jesus came back then, he encountered/befriended . . .

- lepers
- the poor
- women who were mistreated
- public sinners (tax collectors, prostitutes, etc.)
- Samaritans

Feedback and Conclusion

(about 10 minutes)

1. Ask the participants to turn to page 24 in their books, "What I Know Now, I Didn't Know Before." Briefly explain the exercise. Allow the participants five minutes to complete.
2. When everyone has finished, put the slips of paper with the biblical names in a pile where all can see. Shuffle conspicuously and draw one name. Say (for example):

   > Amos, tell us one practical skill or lesson you learned at this session for starting a friendship or building a relationship.

   Repeat the process with other participants as time allows. Comment as necessary. For example:

   > In building any positive relationship, the learning never stops. We may have learned more about each other and about Jesus at this session, but we've just touched the tip of the iceberg. To know Jesus better, we must keep reading about him, asking questions about him, and (especially) talking and listening to him in prayer.

Mentor Meeting Reminder

3. Preview Teen-Mentor Meeting 2 (pages 25-26 in the Participant Book). Offer specific directions as needed. Have the participants record any messages to the mentors in the Mentor Memo panel. Remind them to bring their book to the meeting and to complete the required summary page as assigned.

Jesus, What Do You Stand For?

Objectives

The purpose of this session is to help the participants:

- examine the core theme of Jesus' message—to "reform your lives"—and gain an understanding of how Jesus' message of reform radically challenges the status quo of our lives and the world;
- identify the teachings of Jesus that are the hardest to understand and accept;
- explore a process for incorporating new ideas into beliefs and skills.

Overview

Repentance is an attitude associated with sinfulness, and therefore, often thought to be difficult and avoidable. In fact, a person's repentance is a beautiful initial sign of conversion to a new and different way of life. In a Christian understanding, repentance has to do with a reshaping or reforming of one's life in a radical way from what the world deems important to what is valued according to the words and actions of Jesus. This section focuses on this call of Jesus to repent—for our purposes, to reform our lives—and begin again anew. Several techniques are used in this session. The participants survey the values of today's consumer society by looking through newspaper and magazine articles and advertisements for examples of what the world stands for. To compare, the participants look at several gospel teachings of Jesus. They reflect more closely on what it means to reform one's own life. Many examples of the difficulty of this challenge are presented. In prayer, the participants hear again Jesus' invitation to them to come and follow. In total, this session helps the participants be more aware of what accepting that invitation entails.

Mentor Component

Preview Teen-Mentor Meeting 3 on pages 34-35 of the Participant Book.

Session Outline

Opening Activity: Who's Who? Game (about 20 minutes)

Part I: Jesus' Message . . . No Sugar Added! (about 60 minutes)

Break (about 5 minutes)

Part II: Re-form! How an Idea Became A Belief (about 50 minutes)

Prayer Experience: Jesus Prayer (about 10 minutes)

Conclusion (about 5 minutes)

Supplies

For this session you will need:
- a stack of 3" x 5" pieces of paper
- stick-on notes
- (optional) a photo of a celebrity used in the opening activity
- pens
- two or three rolls of tape
- a supply of magazines and newspapers for each small group table
- a bible marked to the following passages: Is 11:1-8, Lk 4:14-22, Jn 6:60-69
- VCR and monitor
- video clip of several cartoon segments
- (optional) *Gandhi* video set at the point when the young Gandhi attempts to put into practice the Christian notion of "turning the other cheek"
- bibles (New Testament) for each participant
- candle
- an illustration of Jesus and a poster board with the words "Reform Your Lives" written on it
- tape or CD player and recording of reflective music

Special Preparations

1. For the opening activity you will need to prepare stick-on notes (one for each participant) with the names of celebrities who possess a very prominent reputation (for better or worse) in these various fields:
   - politics/government
   - show biz/glamour
   - Wall Street/business/corporate world
   - music

- sports
- notorious underworld figures/criminals
- service/Christian values

The celebrities can be living or dead. You might want to ask a teen who is not taking this course to help you come up with a suitable list.

2. You will need to prepare and edit a ten-minute video of cartoon segments such as the Roadrunner, Tom and Jerry, Ren and Stimpy, Roger Rabbit, etc. that show characters doing things that are unimaginable in real life (i.e., falling off a cliff and walking away unhurt).

Settings

You will need the following areas for this session:
1. A room (with tables and chairs) for gathering that is purposefully too small for your needs.
2. A large group area (with easy access to the first, smaller area) where you can gather the groups in a relaxed and informal atmosphere. There should be viewing access to a board or easel.
3. An area where the participants can meet around tables.
4. (optional) An outdoor space that the entire group will be able to go to for a short portion of the session. The space should be sizable and comfortable.
5. An area for the Prayer Experience. The floor of the church sanctuary often works well. If this area is impossible to use, arrange the large group area into a comfortable setting for prayer.

Opening Activity: Who's Who? Game

(about 20 minutes)

1. As the participants arrive, have them check in with their group moderators and show their Teen-Mentor Meeting 2 summary page and mentor's verification signature.
2. After the check-in, gather the participants in the room that is too small for your needs. Go around the room (the moderators can assist you) and place a stick-on note with a celebrity's name on each person's back. Do not let the participants see their assigned names. Tell them not to tell anyone else his or her assigned name.

Game

3. Ask everyone to sit at one of the tables. Distribute one 3" x 5" piece of paper and a pen to each participant and give the following instructions. Say:

> We are going to begin this session with a game called "Who's Who?" Each of you has a name of a very famous person on your back. We could even say that these people "stand for" or represent certain values, for better or worse. Do not look at your name and do not tell anyone else his or her name. You have also been given a piece of paper and a pen. When we begin, each of you is to walk around and ask another person to look at the name on your back. Ask the person:

"What values do I stand for?" On the piece of paper write down a word or phrase that captures what the other person says. For example, if I had Abraham Lincoln's name on my back, what should be some words and phrases you would use to capture what he stood for (honesty, freedom for all people, courage, leadership, etc.)? Remember, we're not giving clues about a person's profession, but what values they stand for. After you write down what the person says, exchange roles and suggest a word or phrase to represent the values of the person on his or her back. Then move on to another person and repeat the process. Try to write as many clues about your identity as you can. The object is to see if you can guess your celebrity just by looking at the clues for what values they "stand for." Any questions? (Pause to answer.) Begin.

4. Allow enough time for everyone to get a few clues about their identity. Ask those who correctly guess their identities to have a seat. After a few minutes, ask everyone to sit down and check the stick-on note to see who they were. Put the names of two or three of the celebrities on the board (if possible, bring in a photo of a few) and have the participants share some of the various responses that were suggested to describe the values the person(s) stands for.

5. Collect all the discarded stick-on notes. Tell the participants to stay in their places for the start of the next activity.

Part I: Jesus' Message . . . No Sugar Added!

(about 60 minutes)

Grouping

1. Form new groups for this part of the session. Designate tables according to the celebrity categories from the opening activity (i.e., politics, show biz, sports, etc.). Point to a table and say, for example:

    This is the table for music celebrities. Everyone who had a music celebrity on his or her back, come and have a seat at this table. Bring your pen and Participant Book with you. (Repeat the process for as many categories as you had in the opening activity.)

2. Assign an adult to each table. When everyone is in place, introduce the following activity.

Activity

3. Say:

    In our opening activity we had a chance to discuss what some famous people stand for. Our goal in this lesson is to look at what Jesus stands for. But before we do that, let's look at some more of the values of our popular culture. What really matters in the eyes of society? What messages does society give us about what's important and what's not? In other words, what does our world stand for? As a way to answer this question, you are going to spend a few minutes looking through some newspapers and magazines to try to get a handle on the world's values. Look at the headlines. Look at the advertisements. Look at the photos and illustrations. In all cases, keep these questions in mind:

- What does our society count as important?
- What ideas, themes, and messages are being promoted as crucial?
- What does our world stand for?

(Some examples of what the world stands for might be things like power, success, good looks, status, etc. You may need to offer a few of these examples to get things going.)

4. Ask the participants to turn to "What Does the World Stand For," page 28 in their books. Tell them that as they look at headlines, stories, advertisements, and photos they are to write at least five ideas in the space provided.

5. Call on runners from each group to come to the supply table to pick up magazines and newspapers for their tables. Allow about seven minutes for the participants to browse through the material and record their thoughts. Then, say:

Each person share with the group one thing he or she believes the world stands for. The person wearing the most red can go first. If you have time, go around again and share a second thing.

6. After the groups have had enough time for discussion, call on one person from each group (the one wearing the most red) to offer one or two points of summary. List these "worldly values" on the board. Point to the list and comment how the items provide a summary of what people deem important. Make sure that the participants understand that everyone, to a degree, attaches value to the things that are listed on the board. Then, continue your talk based on the following script.

Script

7. Let's begin to contrast the items on the list by looking at what Jesus stands for. Rather than look at newspapers or magazines, let's look at another written source: the gospels! The very first public words and actions of Jesus recorded in the gospel of Matthew tell us a great deal about Jesus and what he values. They say:

"Jesus began to preach and say, 'Repent, for the kingdom of heaven is at hand'" (4: 17).

Repent is a word that often gets a bad rap. You may associate it with punishment to fit a crime—kind of like detention is to cutting a class. But repent means much more. It actually is closely associated with the word reform. Other translations of the Bible have quoted Jesus as saying, "Reform your lives." What associations come to mind when you hear the word reform? (Pause to allow volunteers to comment.)

> If the author of Matthew's gospel had been a campaign manager for Jesus, he might have chosen to use the word reform on all of his campaign posters. For our purposes, we're going to start with the idea of reform as the central idea that Jesus stands for. In order to get a better understanding of what Jesus means by reform, let's begin with an experiment.

8. Comment on how cramped the room is and how a better arrangement is needed. Ask the participants to rearrange the furniture in the room to accomplish some improvement. Allow one minute to rearrange the room (treating the furniture with respect of course). After a minute, have everyone sit and look around. Ask them if they like the new arrangement. Insist that you are not satisfied and instruct them to try rearranging again for another minute. Repeat this process a third time. Finally, after the third time, tell everyone that you don't see any point in this. Rearranging the room in a number of ways simply does not make the conditions any better! Next, motion the group to follow you to the second, larger room that you have prepared (or, if weather permits, outdoors). When you arrive at the new place, ask volunteers to compare some differences in the two spaces. Invite someone to recap what the group had just done. For example:
   - arrived and participated in activity in a small room, with furniture that was inadequately arranged;
   - rearranged the furniture several times with no real improvement;
   - left the small room altogether and went into this new, very large space, totally different from the small room we started in.
   - Continue the lesson from the script.

Script (continued)

9. Say:

   > Rearranging the same furniture in the same inadequate room gets pretty boring after a while. It just doesn't lead anywhere. In much the same way, we often do this with our lives. We just keep rearranging the same thoughts, ideas, relationships, and so on without any real improvement. When Jesus talks about reforming our lives, he's not talking about trying a new fad, losing a few pounds, rehabilitating a bad habit. Re-forming our lives in Jesus means entering into a whole new space, a whole new reality, a whole new way of being. When Jesus tells us to reform our lives he really means to reshape, rebuild, overhaul, turn upside down and inside out. That's very dramatic. Jesus literally asks us to be "born again" as a person, to leave the old self behind and follow him. Let's try to find out how Jesus expects us to do this.

Exercise

10. Give the participants these directions. Say:

    > I'm going to read something you might find peculiar. I want you to listen for two things. First, about half-way through you'll hear me mention a lot of animals. Try to remember the kinds of animals you hear. Second, try to remember which animals are described as being paired together.

Read Isaiah 11:1-8 with emphasis on verses 6-8 ("the wolf shall be a guest of the lamb" etc.). Call on volunteers to share what animals were mentioned and how they paired up.

Answers:

wolf/lamb
leopard/kid
calf/young lion/little child
cow/bear
lion/ox
baby/cobra
child/adder

Ask:

> What do you find peculiar about the way the animals are paired together?

11. Allow two or three volunteers the chance to comment. Then, continue:

> The images in that passage may call to mind the implausibility of animals running amok in a Loony Tunes cartoon! Actually, the prophet Isaiah used that kind of imagery to describe how God's kingdom will be reformed at the coming of the Messiah. And, Jesus reiterated the point himself when he read from the very same prophet Isaiah in his first public appearance at his hometown synagogue in Nazareth. Listen to what Jesus said and to what happened next. (Read Lk 4:14-22.) Jesus is telling the people "you know how Isaiah described a time when the Messiah will come and turn the world upside down and inside out? Well, here I am!" You can imagine why the people were so shocked and upset. Jesus was the kid down the block, someone they had watched grow up in their own town. For him to claim to be the Messiah—well, it was so astonishing to them that they forced him out of the synagogue and to the edge of town where they tried to throw him head first over a cliff. (Read Lk 4:28 to emphasize.)
>
> The reaction of the townspeople of Nazareth was typical of the reactions to many people since who find out what Jesus really stands for: Reform! Turning your life upside down and inside out. In other words, not just rearranging furniture.

Video Presentation/Activity

12. Tell the participants to open their books to page 29, "Cartoons: Turning the World Upside Down and Inside Out." Prepare to show a ten-minute collection of edited cartoon segments (Roadrunner, Tom and Jerry, Roger Rabbit, etc.) that depict characters doing things that are not humanly possible (i.e., falling off cliffs, getting blown up and yet still surviving). Explain the directions. Make sure the participants know that they are to jot down notes as the video is being shown. After the video, elicit a list of all the things the participants saw cartoon characters doing that are humanly impossible. Say:

> One reason that cartoons are entertaining is that they are an escape from reality. Actually they invite us to enter another "reality" where animals can talk and

people can fly and both of them can be blown to bits and get right back up without even a scratch! Cartoons are an example of something that turns our world upside down and inside-out. As strange as it may seem, there are similarities in the message of Jesus. In fact, the very notion of turning the world upside down and inside out is at the heart of the gospel message. It's what Jesus' message is all about. When Jesus asks us to follow him, it's not a token invitation. He's asking us:

- Are you willing to change your vision and see life in a totally different way?
- Are you willing to let your world be turned upside down and inside out? In other words, are you ready to be a part of a world in which the poor are blessed? mourners are comforted? the other cheek is turned? prayer is offered for those who hurt us? enemies are loved? the first are last and the last are first? the greatest among you wash the feet of the least?

That doesn't sound like the world we described in the Opening Activity. Rather, by his invitation, Jesus is asking you to base your life on some new, different, and strange (by the world's standards) ideas. It's no doubt a scary proposition. And it's definitely not an easy one. After a five-minute break return to your same small group table. We'll look at some of the ideas Jesus has that would turn our world upside down and inside out and at how we can possibly take him seriously.

Break

(about 5 minutes)

Allow a brief time for a stretch, drink of water, etc. Tell the participants to bring their book, a pen, and a bible with them to their small group table after the break.

Part II:
Re-form! How an Idea Became a Belief

(about 50 minutes)

1. After the group has assembled at the small group tables, begin the lesson with a summary of the material covered before the break. Say:

    What does Jesus stand for? Our first clue to answering this question is the word *reform*. We admitted before the break that taking Jesus' ideas seriously and making them a part of our lives is a difficult undertaking. How is it done? Open your books to page 30, "Trying Something New" to get a clue about how to translate ideas into belief.

2. Read the directions on page 30 of the Participant Book. Have the participants write their names, addresses, and phone numbers in their very best handwriting in the left column. They should then write the same information with their off hand in the right column. After most have finished, ask them to pass their books around the table so that the others can see how they did. Ask volunteers to comment to the large group on the experience (how it felt to write with the off hand) and describe their finished product (sloppy, sick, terrible, a mess, etc.). Focus at-

tention on the idea of why it is so difficult to try something one way when we are accustomed to doing it another way. Say:

> When we are accustomed to doing things one way, it is difficult to get used to a new way. The idea of doing something we've always done in a new and different way may at first seem ridiculous. A complete waste of time. Even if we are willing to try, the experience might seem frustrating and awkward. It's only with much practice that we can eventually achieve some success. Let's look at some other examples of reforming old habits into new skills.

3. Brainstorm and discuss some examples with the group. Invite the participants to tell stories of actual experiences and feelings of learning or reforming some new skills. For example:
   - a baby learns to walk after months of crawling;
   - a teen learns to roller-blade after months of roller-skating (If space and conditions permit, invite someone to try roller-blading for the first time!);
   - a football player switches positions from offense to defense;
   - a student moves to a foreign country and has to communicate in a new language.

4. Determine with the group a list of essentials for mastering new skills or techniques. Write (and save) the list on the board. It may include:
   - trial and error
   - learning from mistakes
   - practice, practice, practice
   - determination
   - stick-to-itivenss
   - support and encouragement from others when the going gets rough

Say:

> If I am a ten-month-old baby, I would say that crawling is just fine, thank you! The idea of moving around on my feet seems crazy (for a baby, feet are better for chewing on)! Why should I go through all the trouble of falling down and banging my head and my legs and my arms and my hands?
>
> Babies learning to walk can get very frustrated, but they will also keep trying because they sense with every small step that they are on to a life that offers many more possibilities than before. For teens, learning to drive can be a hassle. There are driver's education classes to take, behind-the-wheel training to perform, tests to pass. But most teens are willing to put up with all of this because they sense that with gaining a driver's license and being able to drive a car, a whole new reality will open for them. And, they're right!
>
> Likewise, Jesus' call to reform our lives seems difficult and hardly worth the bother at first. You may be wondering:

- Why should I turn the other cheek when an eye-for-an-eye seems more fair?
- Why should I love my enemies when they will continue to hate me?
- Why should I rejoice when I'm persecuted when feeling sorry for myself seems to make more sense?

5. Point out that these are just a few of the challenges of following Jesus. Have the participants open their books to page 31, "Jesus, You've Got to Be Kidding!" to uncover some other challenges of discipleship. Allow about fifteen minutes for the participants to browse through the passages listed (either individually, with a partner, or with the small group) and write a list of the ideas that they find very difficult to understand or accept. Then, say:

> Share the passage, teaching, or idea associated with Jesus that you find most difficult with your group. The person who looks most perplexed can go first.

After about ten minutes, call on one person in each group to summarize some of the things that were shared. (Write them on the board.) Then, continue:

> These are the answers to the question "Jesus, what do you stand for?" (point to the list). Yet, we find many of them difficult to understand or accept. What are we supposed to do about this? Do we just give up? Do we stop following Jesus altogether? Do we ignore his teachings? Do we give them lip-service? Do we sugarcoat them?

Refer to the list of essentials for mastering new skills or techniques (see no. 4, above). Ask if that advice applies to following Jesus and his teachings. Take one of Jesus' teachings and discuss how one of the items on the list can be helpful. Repeat with the other essentials as time permits.

Optional: Show a video segment from the beginning of the motion picture Gandhi in which the young Gandhi attempts to put into practice the Christian notion of turning the other cheek (about five minutes).

Journal Activity

6. As a summary to this lesson, have the participants follow the directions on pages 32-33, "Jesus Roadblocks" and complete each of the suggestions. Play a reflective instrumental piece as background music while the group is working. Allow about ten minutes.

Prayer Experience: Jesus Prayer

(about 10 minutes)

1. Ask the participants to bring their books and move to the area you have reserved for the Prayer Experience. Ask the group to sit in a circle. Turn down the lights and place a lighted candle in the center of the room. After the group is quieted

proceed immediately with a reading from John 6:60-69. (You may wish to choose another adult to do this reading.) Then, say:

> In every age those who hear Jesus' words have found them life-giving, yet difficult and hard. Many have chosen to follow Jesus. Others have chosen to go away. Those who have made the choice to follow Jesus have found their lives turned upside down. Reform has often meant living lives poor in spirit, poor in belongings. Reform has often meant forgiving someone who has done them great harm, embracing someone once considered an enemy. Reform has often meant giving up homes, relatives, possessions, and dreams to live a life based on a promise of life with God, a life without end.

2. Play a recording (or arrange for live music, if possible) of some reflective background music. Lead the following form of the meditative "Jesus Prayer." Say:

> We call on Jesus to be with us now. We will recite a rhythmic prayer to help us put ourselves in Jesus' presence. As you inhale, recite the words "Come, Lord Jesus." As you exhale, recite the words "live in me." After our meditation, we will sit quietly and reflect on being in company with Jesus. During the quiet time, you can pray the prayer you wrote to Jesus in your journal activity or any other thoughts that come to mind.

Develop a prayerful rhythm with the Jesus Prayer as above until all have joined in. After the music is over, allow four or five minutes for silent prayer.

Conclusion

(about 5 minutes)

Mentor Meeting Reminder

1. Preview Teen-Mentor Meeting 3 (pages 34-35 in the Participant Book). Offer specific directions as needed. Have the participants record any messages to the mentors in the Mentor Memo panel. Remind them to take their book to the meeting and to complete the required summary by the time that it is due.

2. Conclude the session by saying:

> You've been given a challenge to follow Jesus more closely. What does reform mean for you? Take some time to think about this on your own. Talk to Jesus in prayer. Recall what he stands for. Ask yourself if you want to stand with him. If the idea of moving into a whole new reality, of discovering different ways to look at the world appeals to you, you are ready for the next session. If you just want to hear more about Jesus and the challenge of reform, you're welcome too. See you next time!

Session Four

Jesus, When Do You Speak to Me?

Objectives

The purpose of this session is to help the participants:
- recognize personal "aha" experiences; that is, times they have gained new insight into something that may have once seemed ordinary;
- find Jesus in many different people, places, and situations;
- explore how Jesus used parables to engage people, present them with the unexpected, and lead them to reform their lives.

Overview

It's surprising to find out that many practicing and committed Christians have trouble naming times when they have experienced Jesus' presence in a personal way. Jesus' presence in word, sacrament, and community is well chronicled. But it takes a bit of personal insight for anyone to recognize Jesus in these and other places and to be able to name how Jesus "speaks to me." Everyone has had some insightful experience. In this session the participants define such times and recall how the experience led them to look at something or someone in a new way. They are asked to do the same as far as their understanding of how Jesus speaks to them, both through everyday people and events and through the creative, timeless medium of the parables he told. Finally, they are asked to write about how a parable of Jesus is calling them to reform.

Mentor Component

Preview Teen-Mentor Meeting 4 on pages 43-44 of the Participant Book. Pay special attention to Activity Suggestion 2. Arrange with a local soup kitchen or homeless shelter for opportunities for mentors and teens to volunteer. (You may want to assign this project to the entire group.)

Session Four

Session Outline

Opening Activity: Team Charades (about 30 minutes)
Part I: The "Aha" Moments: Stories of Insight (about 40 minutes)
Break (about 5 minutes)
Part II: Parables: Recipes for Insight and Reform (about 45 minutes)
Prayer Experience: One Body, One Spirit (about 20 minutes)
Feedback and Conclusion (about 10 minutes)

Supplies

For this session you will need:
- masking tape
- a stack of 3" x 5" cards for charades
- one copy of Resource 5, 6, and 7, pages 128-130, for each small group table
- (optional) an enlargement or transparency of Resource 7, page 130
- (optional) overhead projector
- pens
- copies of Resource 8, "Brain Teasers" (one for each participant)
- dark-colored crayons or fine tipped markers
- tape or CD player and recording of reflective music
- strips of light-colored cloth (3" x 20")
- a bible marked to the following passages: Mt 13:10-17 and Eph 4:1-6
- bibles for each participant

Special Preparations

1. You will need to write one phrase on each 3" x 5" card to be used for a game of charades. For example:
   - a father waiting impatiently for, and then being handed, his newborn child
   - Santa and his reindeer landing on the roof
   - the Beast being transformed into a prince
   - the crowd standing for the seventh inning stretch at a baseball game
   - an actor (or actress) winning the Academy Award
   - the pope blessing the crowd at St. Peter's square

2. For the Prayer Experience, write your name on a strip of light-colored cloth. On the other side of the cloth, write a statement or phrase that summarizes the meaning of a favorite parable or how the parable calls you to reform.

Settings

You will need the following areas for this session:
1. A large group area where you can gather the groups in a relaxed and informal atmosphere. Designate several small-group areas (enough room for five or six participants) on the floor by marking them off with masking tape. There should be viewing access to a board or easel.
2. An area where the participants can meet around tables.
3. "Alone" spots—places where the participants can be at least six feet away from anyone else.
4. An area for the Prayer Experience. The floor of the church sanctuary often works well. If this area is impossible to use, arrange the large group area into a comfortable setting for prayer.

Opening Activity: Team Charades

(about 30 minutes)

1. As the participants arrive, have them check in with their group moderators. They should be prepared to show their Teen-Mentor Meeting 3 summary page and mentor's verification signature, if due. After the check-in, the participants should move to the large group meeting area and sit on the floor in one of the areas that has been marked with tape. Have them bring a pen and their books.
2. After everyone has arrived, re-arrange participants to different small group areas of the floor as you see fit. Then, begin by reviewing some of what was covered in Session Three. Call on volunteers to answer one or more of the following questions:
   - What is one gospel passage that you find especially difficult to follow?
   - In one sentence, tell what Jesus "stands for."
   - Share a strategy you learned from your mentor for following Jesus.

Game

3. Have the participants remain in their spaces on the floor. Gather the set of charade cards (one for each group) that were prepared beforehand (see Special Preparations, No. 1). Tell the group you are going to play a game of team charades. Say:

   > In my hand I have a set of cards. On each card is a phrase like "John eating a giant banana split with a fork." Each team will pick one of the cards and will have three minutes to decide how to act out the phrase so that the rest of us can guess what the card says. You may use actions, sounds, and gestures, but you may not use words. Every member of your group should have a part in your presentation. The phrase must be guessed exactly.

Jesus, Should I Follow You?

4. Hold the cards face down, and ask the small groups to send a representative to pick one. Allow about three minutes for the groups to decide how they will present their phrases. (If the marked-off spaces are too close to one another, allow the groups to move to various corners of the room where they will not be heard by the other groups.)

5. Call the groups back together and select one group to do the first presentation. Pay special attention to the excitement in a person when they get a flash of insight and guess the right answer.
   Optional: Keep track of the group that solves the most phrases. Award a prize (candy, cookies, etc.) to the members of the winning group.

Part I:
The "Aha" Moments: Stories of Insight

(about 40 minutes)

1. Tell the groups to remain in their designated areas (in or around the marked-off spaces on the floor). Say:

   > People have played various forms of charades for many years. It's a fun party game. But an element of charades makes an important point that we are going to delve into a little deeper at this session. More on that later. First, I'm going to ask you to participate in an experiment.

2. Distribute one copy of Resource 5 (the young woman), page 128, to each of the small groups on one side of the room. Distribute one copy of Resource 6 (the old woman), page 129, to each of the small groups on the other side of the room. Do not let the groups on one side of the room see the other side's pictures. Instruct the groups to put their picture on the floor in the center of their group, huddle closely, and concentrate on the image (in silence) for ten to fifteen seconds. Then collect all the copies.

3. Pass out one copy of Resource 7 (the combination of the old/young woman), page 130, to all the groups. (Or, project an overhead transparency or hold up an enlargement of Resource 7 for all to see.) Ask the groups to describe what they see and, in particular, the age of the woman. Invariably, most will see what they were "conditioned" to see and not the "other woman." When this happens, allow participants to mingle from group to group to point out the features of the woman (young or old) that they see. Again, note moments of insight when someone's eyes are opened to see the picture in a different way. After everyone has been clued-in, ask them to have a seat near you and the board. Prepare some introductory words to the lesson based on the following script:

Script

4. Most of you saw this last picture in the way you had been conditioned to see it. However, when challenged to see the picture in another way, a flash of insight occurred. (Write **insight** on the board. Point out one or two of the specific moments of insight that you witnessed; for example, "When Erica recognized the old woman she let out a loud 'Aha . . . now I see it!'".) It's that flash of insight that leads us to look at something in an entirely different way.

> Think back to the game of team charades. It was a similar experience. The phrase was a mystery to you until you were given enough clues. Then, suddenly, the so-called light bulb went on for someone in your group and he or she shouted out the right answer. From your reactions I could tell that discovering something that was previously a mystery is exciting!
>
> All of this has a great deal to do with understanding how Jesus speaks to us and how we hear him. In Session Three we looked at what Jesus stands for and we focused our attention on his call to reform our lives and re-shape our way of looking at things. Yet, to do that, it takes a major moment of insight or what is sometimes called an "Aha!" experience for us to go from seeing life one way to looking at it in an entirely new way. Let's look at some other examples of "Aha!" experiences.

5. Tell the participants to open their books to page 37, "Now I Get It!" and to individually read the two scenarios at the top of the page. Allow two or three minutes and then continue by asking the following questions:
   - What are some insights Tony gained from his experience? (his mother's deep concern for his health and safety, her ability to express her love for him, etc.)
   - What are some insights Marla gained from her experience? (how much she valued her grandmother, a deeper significance of Grandma's garden)

6. Expand on the notion of insight and how taking a fresh look can help us to see our relationships with others in a new way. Ask how this might be true in the way we relate to Jesus. Have the participants read the list of situations described on the bottom of page 37 and tell where Jesus' presence might be seen in each. Then ask them to complete the Journal Activity that follows on page 38.

7. Ask each person to share with their small group one insight they wrote about Jesus in the Journal Activity (the person with the longest hair can go first). Allow five or six minutes. Then call on one person from each group to summarize what was said. Record some of the insights on the board. Then say:

> Jesus communicates to us in many ways. All we need to do is open our eyes and take notice. Another way that Jesus communicates to us is through his word in the gospels. After the break we will examine how Jesus communicates to us in a story form called parables.

Break

(about 5 minutes)

Allow a brief time for a stretch, drink of water, etc. Tell the participants to meet with their same groups at a table with a bible, book, and pen after the break.

Part II:
Parables: Recipes for Insight and Reform

(about 45 minutes)

1. When the groups have reassembled at tables, distribute one copy of Resource 8, "Brain Teasers," page 131, to each participant. Tell them to work as a group and solve as many brain teasers as they can in five minutes.

2. Call time after five minutes and go over the correct answers:

Answers
    1a. Much Ado About Nothing
    1b. World Without End, Amen
    1c. A frame-up
    1d. Hole in one
    1e. Six of one, half a dozen of another
    1f. Happy meal

    2a. deed
    2b. noon
    2c. sexes
    2d. civic
    2e. rotator

    3a. bikini
    3b. dividing
    3c. illicit
    3d. inclining
    3e. limiting
    3f. visibility
    3g. missing
    3h. Mississippi
    3i. timidity

3. Collect the resource sheets and continue the lesson based on the following script. (A board should be in view of the entire group; if necessary, ask the participants to move to the large group area.)

Script

4. Whether you like or dislike brain teasers, whether you are good at solving them or not, brain teasers are very engaging; that is, once you are challenged to solve one, it's difficult to let go of it until you have found the right answer.

Jesus used a form of storytelling called **parables** (write on the board) that had a similar effect on people as a brain teaser: after you hear a parable you have to figure out its meaning for yourself. Let's look at some of the characteristics of parables:

Parables include **common experiences** (write) that everyone can understand and relate to. Jesus didn't use space aliens or angels as central characters. He used people. His parables featured settings, materials, and situations that people in every generation can understand.

A brain teaser has one, definitive answer. Parables, too, illustrate a **single point** (write). Though the meaning of a parable is not meant to be complicated, it is often **unexpected** (write). One of the interesting characteristics of Jesus' parables are the inclusion of a surprising twist: for example, in the parable of the Lost (Prodigal) Son, it's surprising and unexpected that the father would throw a party for a son who had abandoned the family and blown all of his inheritance.

Parables are also truly **interactive** (write) in the sense that they engage the listeners to struggle with the story until they find the meaning. And, once the meaning has been found, they are further engaged to figure out how the meaning could possibly apply to them.

Exercise

5. Tell the participants that they are going to read one or more parables and discuss the follow-up questions with their groups. Ask them to open their books to page 39-40, "Parables of Jesus." Assign each group one parable to begin with. Move around the room and provide help with the "meaning of the parable" if asked. Allow about fifteen minutes. If a group finishes reading and discussing one parable, have them continue with the others.

6. Call time and ask the participants to turn to page 41, "A Call to Reform" Say:

    In his parables Jesus doesn't just speak to the world of two thousand years ago or to a select group of church leaders or to the person next to you. The meaning of the parables is intended especially for you! It is a personal call to you to help you to reform your life and live in a new, different, and unexpected way. I would like you to spend some quiet time thinking on your own about Jesus' parables and how they might be addressed to you today. For the exercise on page 41-42, you will move to an "alone" spot. Take a bible and quietly read or re-read the parables listed on page 39-40, listening for a message from Jesus. Write one parable that has special meaning for you. Then complete questions 2 and 3.

    Allow ten to fifteen minutes. When the time is up, ask the group to bring their books with them to the area you have reserved for the Prayer Experience.

Prayer Experience: One Body, One Spirit

(about 20 minutes)

1. Gather the participants into a large circle on the floor. Distribute a strip of light-colored cloth (3" x 20") and a dark-colored crayon or fine-tipped marker to each person. Say:

    > Write your name on one side of the cloth. On the other side, write a statement or phrase that summarizes the meaning of one of the parables you heard for you or how the parable is calling you to reform. (Demonstrate with a cloth you have prepared for yourself.) During this prayer time you will be asked to briefly explain what you have written.

2. Play some reflective music to initiate an atmosphere of prayer. Allow three to four minutes for the participants to complete their cloths. Collect the crayons and have everyone sit on the floor and form a circle. Take a bible marked with Matthew 13:10-17 (the purpose of parables) and sit in the middle of the circle. After one or two minutes of silence, begin by reading the scripture passage to the group. Then, say:

    > The apostles were having trouble understanding Jesus' parables. They were becoming rather irritated and tired of the brain teasers. They asked Jesus why he taught in parables. Couldn't he speak clearer? Jesus' response, which we just heard, still sounds rather confusing. Actually, what Jesus is saying is that in order to understand parables, we must reflect on their meaning. And, after we reflect and understand the meaning, we must reform our lives according to what we have been called to do.
    >
    > Each of you has had a chance to reflect on the meaning of a parable for your own life. You have thought about how the parable is calling you to reform. When it is your turn, share with the group something you found meaningful and/or how the meaning of the parable has inspired you to reform your life. When you are done sharing, tie the end of your cloth strip to the strip of the person next to you. That is the cue for that person to share. The person on my right will begin.

3. After everyone has shared, ask the group to stand (the cloths should form the appearance of a wreath). Say:

    > Each of us hears Jesus speaking to us in different ways. Each of us is called to reform our lives in different ways. However, one thing ties us together: the fact that Jesus speaks to each of us in a personal way. All of our individual stories are tied together in Jesus to make one great story of our unity in him.

4. Pass the marked bible to a good reader. Ask him or her to conclude the prayer by reading Ephesians 4:1-6 (unity in the mystical body).

Feedback and Conclusion

(about 10 minutes)

Mentor Meeting Reminder

1. Preview Teen-Mentor Meeting 4 (see pages 43-44 in the Participant Book). Point out the activity suggestions to the participants. If you have arranged for a time and place for the teens and mentors to do a service project (see Activity Suggestion 2), have the participants record the information in the Mentor Memo panel to be shared with their mentors.
2. Ask: "What is one new insight you gained at this session?" Call on volunteers to respond.
3. Dismiss the group on time.

Jesus, What Do You Do For Me?

session Five

Objectives

The purpose of this session is to help the participants:
- identify the truth in the old saying "actions speak louder than words";
- witness how Jesus used dramatic actions to communicate important teachings;
- understand the nature of the miracle stories in the gospels and how actions elicit reactions.

Overview

Session Four focused attention on how Jesus speaks to us in words, specifically through parables. In this session the participants will continue to explore Jesus' call to new life through insight and reform, but this time the focus will be on several of Jesus' miracles as recorded in the gospels. The participants will be reminded how actions can be used to express things much differently (and often better) than words alone do. Jesus used actions several times to add dramatic punch to his teachings. The participants explore the teachings and actions associated with the healing of a paralytic, the raising of Lazarus, and the washing of the disciples' feet. Actions lead to reactions; the session examines the reactions of those who witnessed Jesus' miracles and helps the participants consider how they, personally, react to what Jesus said and did. In prayer, the participants reflect on the ways that Jesus continues to act dramatically in the life of the world today.

Mentor Component

Preview Teen-Mentor Meeting 5 on pages 53-54 of the Participant Book. Activity Suggestion 2 recommends doing service work with the blind, deaf, or physically challenged. To help facilitate this option, arrange with a local agency for groups of teens and mentors to visit and spend some time ministering to and with its clients.

Session Outline

Opening Activity: Guess What Simon Says (about 15 minutes)
Part I: Actions Speak Louder Than Words (about 45 minutes)
Prayer Experience: Signs and Wonders (about 15 minutes)
Break (about 5 minutes)
Part II: How Do You React? (about 60 minutes)
Feedback and Conclusion (about 10 minutes)

Supplies

For this session you will need:
- (optional) prize(s) for the winner(s) of the Opening Activity game
- a copy of Resource 9, "Scripture Cards" (cut apart on dashed lines)
- small paper cups
- video of *Oh God!* set near the conclusion (at the beginning of the trial scene)
- VCR and monitor
- bibles for each participant
- candle
- smaller candle and wax holder for each participant
- tape or CD player and recording of reflective music
- a stack of feedback slips (3" x 5" slips of paper)
- bible marked to the following passage: Mk 6:7-13, 30

Special Preparation

Prepare five solution keys on index cards to help facilitate the game of "Simon Says" (see Opening Activity, No. 4).

Settings

You will need the following areas for this session:
1. A large group area where you can gather the groups in a relaxed and informal atmosphere. There should be an open space in the center or front of the room where small groups can play a version of "Simon Says" and present skits they have prepared. There should be viewing access to a board or easel.
2. An area where the participants can meet around tables.
3. "Alone" spots—places where the participants can sit at least six feet away from anyone else.
4. An area for the Prayer Experience. The floor of the church sanctuary often works well. If this area is impossible to use, arrange the large group area into a comfortable setting for prayer.

Opening Activity: Guess What Simon Says

(about 15 minutes)

1. Welcome the participants as they arrive. Ask them to check in with their group moderators and show their Teen-Mentor Meeting 4 summary sheet and verification signature. After checking-in, the participants can assemble in the large group meeting area and wait for further directions.

Game

2. Use the "count off" method to divide the participants into four groups. First, designate four adult judges (or four of the participants if there are not enough adults). Then, have the participants count off from one to four. Have all the "ones" line-up horizontally facing the board. (The groups can sit while you explain the directions.) Their judges should take a spot at the end of their rows. The twos, threes, and fours take their places in lines directly behind the ones. The pattern should look like this:

```
              Board
J  1  1  1  1  1  1  1  1
J  2  2  2  2  2  2  2  2
J  3  3  3  3  3  3  3  3
J  4  4  4  4  4  4  4
```

3. Explain the directions for a game called Guess What Simon Says. Say:

> This game is almost like the traditional "Simon Says", except for one catch. You have to guess the action I want you to perform, like jumping up and down, by a word I say, like umbrella. Except for use in this game, "umbrella" really doesn't have anything to do with "jumping up and down," so you really have to pay attention when I go over the pattern so that you will know what action you are to do. Also, like the traditional game, make sure that I preface my directions with "Simon says . . ." Your judge at the end of the row will be watching for goof-ups. When you're out, take a seat at the side of the game so that you can watch us try to determine a champion.

4. Write the five actions the participants will be asked to perform on the board. As you *write* each action, *say* loud and clear the clue word (in parenthesis) that is associated with it:
   - **jump up and down** (umbrella)
   - **pat your head** (pencil)
   - **wave hello** (shoes)
   - **stand on one foot** (hat)
   - **whistle** (apple)

Go over the clue words again. Point to the action on the board as you say the clue word. Repeat a third time if you think it's necessary. Then erase the board.

5. Distribute clue cards to the judges. Keep one for yourself. The judges don't play in the game. Rather, they watch the players in their row. When someone messes up, the judges call them out of the game. (Remember, when "Simon says" is omitted no one should move.) Ask everyone to stand up and begin the game. Suggested order (increase the speed as the game progresses):

> Simon says pencil (pat your head).
>
> Simon says apple (whistle).
>
> Simon says umbrella (jump up and down).
>
> Simon says shoes (wave hello).
>
> Hat.
>
> Simon says shoes (wave hello).
>
> Simon says umbrella (jump up and down).
>
> Simon says hat (stand on one foot).
>
> Pencil.
>
> Simon says apple (whistle).

Repeat as often as necessary. Award a prize to the winner. (Round of applause will also do.)

Part I:
Actions Speak Louder Than Words

(about 45 minutes)

1. Ask everyone to sit near the board with their books and pens. Re-cap the game and introduce the lesson. Say:

> In any form of "Simon Says", actions definitely go hand-in-hand with the words. In fact, you couldn't play the game without both the words and the actions.
>
> We live in a world that is very aware of the importance of actions. For example, at one time or another, the following have been popular sayings:
> - Talk is cheap.
> - Walk your talk.
> - Actions speak louder than words.
>
> In Session Four, we examined the significance of Jesus' words, especially his parables. In this session we want to pay special attention to the actions of Jesus that accompanied his words. You are probably already familiar with many of Jesus' actions. Turn to pages 45-46 in your Participant Book. Read the introductory text and then see how many of the actions of Jesus you can identify from the sketches. Take a couple of minutes to share with a person seated near you the meaning or story associated with each of these actions.

2. Allow four to five minutes for sharing. Then continue:

   > The actions associated with each of the gospel stories help us to recall an important lesson associated with Jesus. Actions are also part of our own everyday experiences and have likely helped us to express our own feelings or receive someone else's expression of their feelings. Turn to pages 47-48, "Actions Speak Louder" and write an action you associate with each occasion listed.

3. Allow five to six minutes for the participants to complete Part I. Then call on volunteers to share examples of actions for the various occasions. List some examples on the board. Then, say:

   > Recall an action that you did or received that was very meaningful to you. It may be a hug you gave your grandmother as she arrived at the airport for a visit. It may be a birthday card that your little brother or sister made for you in kindergarten. Look at the list you made in Part I to give you some clues. Then write your description of this very meaningful action in Part II.

4. When most everyone is finished writing, call time and ask the participants to share with a person seated near them the meaningful action they wrote about. After a few minutes, ask volunteers to share with the large group something they wrote or heard that was especially meaningful. Then, ask the participants to meet again with the same group they played "Simon Says" with. The adults or judges can help direct the groups to separate places in the room.

Activity

5. Once the groups have reassembled in different areas of the room, say:

   > Words can be strong. Actions can speak even louder. Words and actions together are a very powerful combination. Jesus combined words and actions to communicate messages that are timeless. To illustrate, let's look at some ways to communicate the stories of Jesus we looked at on pages 45-46. Each group will be given a card with (1) the scripture reference for one of Jesus' stories and (2) directions for communicating the story to the rest of the participants. Take some time to plan your presentation according to the directions. Everyone in the group should have a part.

6. Distribute to each group bibles and one scripture card from Resource 9 (give a small paper cup to every two participants in the group that receives Scripture Card 2). Allow about six to eight minutes for the groups to practice a presentation according to the directions on the card. Then gather everyone together. Arrange space for the groups to do their presentations. Call on the groups in order, one at a time.

7. Do not comment on any one presentation until all four have been presented. Then ask the group to share comments on the differences between the four presentations. Draw these comments from the group:

   For the Scripture Card 1 presentation, say:

   > Jesus' words about everlasting life are key to his message of good news. Yet, taken out of the context of Jesus' raising of Lazarus from the dead, they lose quite a bit of their drama.

For the Scripture Card 2 presentation, say:

> An exchange of water is life-giving. But without hearing Jesus' words to the Samaritan woman, "Whoever drinks the water I shall give will never thirst," we can't understand the breadth of his message.

Regarding the Scripture Card 3 and Scripture Card 4 presentations say:

> Jesus' message packs the most punch when we both hear his words and witness his actions. Words and actions together give us more opportunity to take notice, to pause for thought, to consider what we will do next. Part of the brilliance of Jesus' ministry was that he was able to combine words and actions so effectively in order to teach the truth. Many of Jesus' actions are called miraculous. Because of this we often distance ourselves from them and consider them to be impossible for our own contemporary lives. But should this be so? Let's take some time in prayer to look at how Jesus might be able to perform miracles with us and through us today.

Prayer Experience: Signs and Wonders

(about 15 minutes)

1. Ask the participants to stand up, stretch, and come to the front to pick up a small candle with a wax holder. Then direct them to sit in a circle (either in chairs or on the floor) with their candles, books, and a pen. Light a larger candle and place it in the center of the circle. Begin the prayer experience based on the following script:

Prayer Script

2. > We live in a day and age when miracles seem to be extinct. Science has a way of explaining almost anything that occurs. Things that once might have been considered miracles now have explanations that can be found in any science journal:
>
> - once-deadly diseases (polio, for example) are cured by inoculations or simple treatments;
> - "blindness" is solved by laser cataract surgery, often in just one afternoon's visit;
> - damaged hearts, kidneys, and livers are replaced with others that work better;
> - people who are clinically dead are brought back to life in emergency rooms and kept alive on respirators and with intravenous feedings;
> - space probes uncover much of the mystery of our universe.
>
> With so much of the world explained away, we are conditioned not to expect the surprising, amazing, extraordinary. Most everything becomes commonplace. Actually, if we take a very close look at life around us, we can find much of what can accurately

be termed miraculous, that is, a spontaneous action that could only have its origins in God. Consider the following:
- a woman's inoperable cancerous tumor disappears without medical treatment by the time of her next doctor's visit;
- a man trapped in the rubble of an earthquake is discovered alive nine days later;
- a young woman who had to wear corrective braces on her legs as a child grows up to become an Olympic champion sprinter;
- a man diagnosed with dyslexia perseveres through school, graduates from college, and writes a best-selling novel;
- two sisters at odds with one another for over twenty years reconcile, first by phone call, and then in person over the Christmas holidays.

Of course the list could go on and on. Miracles can be found everywhere. You probably have a personal experience you could term miraculous. With Jesus' help and in Jesus' name, we are all capable of miracles. In fact, the Acts of the Apostles (5:12) reports that "many signs and wonders were done among the people at the hands of the apostles." What signs and wonders might you be called to work in Jesus' name?

What was most miraculous about Jesus was the power he had to change the hearts of people. He used his external miracles to teach us about the more important miracles he wanted to work in people's lives. Blind eyes, deaf ears, and leprous skin were less important to him than spiritual blindness, deafness, and disease.

There are many miracles needed in our lives today, miracles that Jesus can work in us and through us if we give him the chance. We will be moving to our "alone" spots to reflect on some of these, using the exercise "In Jesus' Name," on page 49. (When all are settled in their alone spots, review the directions given on page 49.)

3. Begin the music. Allow five to eight minutes for quiet reflection and writing. Then ask all the participants to stand in a circle with their candles. Say:

    Please share the miracle that you think you are capable of with Jesus' help and the plan you have for enacting it. After you share, light your candle from the center candle and return to the circle. I will go first, anyone can go next.

4. After everyone has shared, read Mark 6:7-13, 30 (mission of the twelve, return of the twelve). Then ask the group to join hands and say an Our Father. After the prayer, dismiss everyone for a five-minute break.

Break

(about 5 minutes)

Allow a brief time for a stretch, drink of water, etc. Tell the participants to meet after the break with their same groups at a table with a bible, book, and pen. A board (or easel) should be in view of all.

Part II: How Do You React?

(about 60 minutes)

1. After the participants have reassembled at a table, tell them you are going to share a mental math problem. Impress on them the importance of listening carefully, staying quiet, and being prepared to move on to each next step. Thoroughly prepare this mental math problem beforehand so that you can move quickly and naturally to each step. (A key to the success of the "trick" is that the listeners don't get a chance to analyze what you are doing.)

Mental Math Problem

2. Present the following problem. Do not read the example. Say:

   > Do each step silently. Don't call out any responses. Don't say anything if you have done this problem before.
   >
   > Think of a number between 1 and 10 (for example, 7).
   >
   > Multiply your number by 9. You now have a two-digit number (for example, 63).
   >
   > Add the two digits of your new number together (for example, 6+3). You now have a one-digit number (9).
   >
   > Subtract 5 from your one-digit number. You now have a new one-digit number (4).
   >
   > Now, pretend each letter of the alphabet corresponds to a number. For example A is 1, B is 2, C is 3, etc. Think of the letter that corresponds to your number (D).
   >
   > Think of a country that starts with your letter (most people will think of Denmark).
   >
   > Now think of an animal that starts with the second letter of your country (most people will think of elephant).

3. Put your hand over your forehead as if some great inspiration is coming to you. Then say, "You are thinking of Denmark and an elephant." There should be varied reactions, for example:
   - "ho-hum" from participants who have done the problem before.
   - confusion from participants who were lost somewhere in the math.
   - amazement from participants who were thinking of Denmark and elephant.

   Note the different reactions by name ("ho-hum," confusion, and amazement). Then, say:

   > One lesson we can draw from this "magic" math game is that an action will elicit a reaction. We spent some time before the break looking at some actions of Jesus known as miracles. In this lesson, we will look at some reactions of people who witnessed Jesus' miracles. As we proceed, take note of how their reactions are similar to those your group had to the "magic" math game ("ho-hum," confusion, amazement).

Jesus, Should I Follow You?

Continue the lesson based on the following script:

Script

4. The miracle stories of Jesus, as they are recorded in the gospels, focus on something Jesus did. They follow a general pattern (write):

   - **There is a problem.**
   - **Jesus solves the problem with a miraculous action.**
   - **People react to the miracle.**

   Think back to the miracle stories we examined in Part I (the raising of Lazarus, the healing of the paralytic). How do these stories fit in the general pattern? (Call on volunteers to suggest ways. Develop and write the following rules on the board.)

   Raising of Lazarus
   Problem: Lazarus had died.
   Miraculous act: Jesus said, "Lazarus come out!" and the dead man came out of the tomb—alive bound in burial wraps.
   Reaction: Some people began to believe in Jesus, others reported his actions to the authorities who wanted to sentence him to death.

   Healing of the Paralytic
   Problem: Man was paralyzed.
   Miraculous act: Jesus healed the man (after forgiving his sins).
   Reaction: Indignation (at Jesus claiming to be able to forgive sins) gave way to amazement after the man was healed.

Exercise

5. Ask the participants to turn to pages 50-52, "Actions and Reactions." Explain the directions for both parts. Make sure the participants understand that they are to work alone on both parts. Move around the room to answer any questions or help with difficulties. Allow about ten minutes. Then, briefly go over the answers to

with difficulties. Allow about ten minutes. Then, briefly go over the answers to Part I:

Answers

The Cure of Simon's Mother-in-Law (Mark 1:29-31)

Problem: Simon's mother-in-law's fever
Miraculous Act: Jesus grasped her hand, helped her up, and the fever left.
Reaction: She waited on them.

The Cleansing of a Leper (Mark 1:40-45)

Problem: Man has leprosy.
Miraculous Act: Jesus said, "Be made clean," and the leprosy left the man.
Reaction: The man told everyone what happened even though Jesus told him not to.

The Healing of a Boy with a Demon (Luke 9:37-43)

Problem: Boy is possessed with a "spirit" that causes him to go into convulsions and to foam at the mouth.
Miraculous Act: Jesus rebuked the spirit and healed the boy.
Reaction: Everyone was amazed.

Video Presentation

6. Before having the participants share their responses to Part II of "Actions and Reactions," prepare to show the conclusion of the video Oh God! beginning with the trial scene (about fifteen minutes). Introduce the video clip. Say:

   > The movie *Oh God!* is a story of miracles and how people react to them. Maybe some of you have seen this movie in which God, played by George Burns, appears to a simple man (John Denver) and asks him to spread the news that God has appeared to him. Naturally most people think he's crazy and they ask that God give some kind of sign. The conclusion of the movie shows some of the ways people react when confronted with the possibility of miracles.

7. After the video, call on volunteers to point out the different reactions of people in the courtroom to the "miracle" that took place. Then say:

   > The crowd that found Jesus "too much" for them wasn't too far off the mark. Jesus' words and actions have tended to bring out strong reactions in people over the generations. People have also found Jesus' words and actions to be confusing, amazing, and difficult to swallow. What about your reaction? Share with your group the reaction to Jesus that you checked on page 52. Explain your choice. The person wearing the most red can go first.

   Allow about ten minutes for sharing. While the groups are sharing, pass out a stack of feedback slips to each table.

Feedback and Conclusion

(about 10 minutes)

1. Write the following sentence starters on the board:

    Something I liked (or didn't like) about this session was . . .

    The most important thing I learned was . . .

    Something Jesus does for me is . . .

2. Instruct each person to complete the three sentences, one on each of three papers. Encourage the participants to sign each paper, but tell them they do not have to do so. Collect the papers. Use them to help you gauge the success of this session and to plan for future sessions.

Mentor Meeting Reminder

3. Preview Teen-Mentor Meeting 5 (see pages 53-54 in the Participant Book). Point out the activity suggestions. If you have arranged for a time and place for the teens and mentors to do a service project (see Activity Suggestion 2), have the participants record the information in the Mentor Memo panel to be shared with their mentors.

4. Remind the group of the date of the next session before dismissing them.

session six

Jesus, What Am I To Do?

Objectives

The purpose of this session is to help the participants:

- contrast the shortcuts to success offered by popular culture with the more difficult costs of following Jesus and embracing his cross;
- identify the sacrifices that go hand in hand with all worthwhile commitments;
- understand the benefits of rising to new life with Jesus.

Overview

This session gets right to the heart of discipleship: following Jesus means dying to self and embracing the cross in the hope of gaining new life. In Part I, the participants are reminded that any goal worth attaining involves sacrifice. The participants examine how this is true for common experiences in their own lives like making a team or being a good friend. However, they also pay close attention to the common human nature that leads people to look for shortcuts and the easy way out in the pursuit of success. This session helps the participants see the worth in the journey itself. A prayer experience asks the participants to commit publicly to "dying to self" in the hope of "rising to new life." Finally, the participants will explore several aspects of Jesus' resurrection and the practical effects the Risen Jesus has on their own lives, now and in the future.

Mentor Component

Preview Teen-Mentor Meeting 6 on pages 61-62 of the Participant Book. Pay special attention to the activity suggestions. Help the teens and mentors arrange opportunities for interviewing the people mentioned in suggestion 3. Also, make known the date, time, and place of events as mentioned in suggestion 2.

Session Six

Session Outline

Opening Activity: The Big Pay-Off (about 25 minutes)
Part I: No Short Cuts Here! (about 50 minutes)
Break (about 5 minutes)
Prayer Experience: Dying and Rising (about 35 minutes)
Part II: Signs of New Life, Signed with New Life (about 30 minutes)
Conclusion (about 5 minutes)

Supplies

For this session you will need:
- pens
- copies of Resource 10, "The Big Pay-Off Tally Sheet," page 133
- copies of Resource 11, "Conversion Speaker Preparation Sheet," page 134
- prize for winning team in the Opening Activity
- crucifix
- video of *Jesus of Nazareth* (Franco Zeferelli) set at the point where Jesus is being scourged by the Roman soldiers
- VCR and monitor
- large cross cut out of poster board
- several popular magazines
- scissors
- glue stick
- candle
- large bowl of holy water
- clean towel for drying hands
- tape or CD player and recording of reflective music
- large electric fan
- bible marked to the following passages:
    Eph 2:1-10; Phil 3:7-16; 1 Cor 15:13-19, 29-32

Special Preparation

Arrange for a guest speaker or a panel of speakers to share with the group experiences of personal conversion. The main point of the talk should be on dying to one's old self and rising again to a new life. Recommendation: Contact a local twelve-step program (for example, Alcoholics Anonymous or Narcotics Anonymous) for possible speakers. Twelve-step programs mirror the notion of dying and rising. Another possibility is to arrange for a mature teen or young adult to speak about a specific conversion experience and about becoming a new person in the Risen Jesus. Offer the speaker(s) a copy of Resource 11, "Conversion Speaker Preparation Sheet," page 134, to help in planning the talk.

Settings

You will need the following areas for this session:
1. A large group area where you can gather the groups in a relaxed and informal atmosphere. There should be viewing access to a board or easel.
2. An area where the participants can meet around tables.
3. An area for the Prayer Experience (optional). The floor of the church sanctuary often works well. If this area is impossible to use, arrange the large group area into a comfortable setting for prayer.
4. "Alone" spots in places where participants can sit at least six feet away from anyone else.

Opening Activity: The Big Pay-Off

(about 25 minutes)

1. Welcome the participants as they arrive. Ask them to check in with their group moderators and show their Teen-Mentor Meeting 5 summary sheet and verification signature, if due. After check-in, the participants should bring their book and a pen and move to the large group area.

Grouping

2. After everyone has arrived, tell each participant to choose a partner. (If there is an odd person left, he or she can be added to one of the pairs.) These pairs will be referred to as a team. Next, arrange four teams together in what will be referred to as a cluster. Form as many clusters as you can. Arrange the seating as follows to reflect the cluster structure:

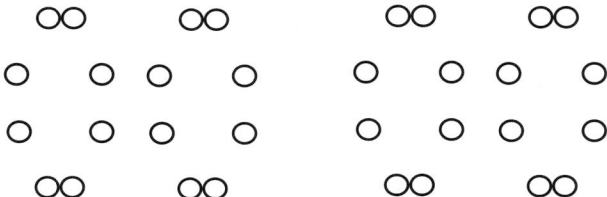

Tables and chairs for each cluster are helpful but not necessary. A comfortable area of the floor is quite adequate.

Game

3. Distribute to each team one copy of Resource 10, "The Big Pay-Off Tally Sheet." Explain the game as follows. Say:

> We are going to play a game called "The Big Pay-Off." The object of the game is for your team to have more "money" on your ledger at the end of the game than any other team. For eight successive rounds, you and your partner decide whether to circle an "A" or a "B" on your tally sheet. The value of the "A" or

"B" is determined by what letters the other teams in your cluster circle. Here's the scoring pattern (write on the board):

4 A's=lose $10　　　**1 A=win $30**
　　　　　　　　　　　3 B's=lose $10

3 A's=win $10
1 B=lose $30　　　**4 B's=win $10**

2 A's=win $20
2 B's=lose $20

4. Play through a sample round so that the participants can get a hang of some of the strategy. Explain that each team will have a minute to confer with one another. One team may decide they want to go for the big pay-off ($30) and circle A. But they note that if the other three teams also circle A they will lose $10. Nevertheless, they circle A. After one minute they are asked to verify their choice with the other teams in the cluster. It turns out that another team marked A but two other teams marked B. That means that the teams that marked As win $20, the teams that marked Bs lose $20. (Point to the scoring key on the board.) The round scores and balance are recorded on the tally sheet.

5. Continue explaining more about the game. Say:

    For each round you will be allowed exactly one minute to discuss with only your partner about which letter to circle for your team. Keep your choice a secret.

    Rounds 4, 6, and 8 will be different, however. They will be bonus rounds with the values being doubled. Also, you will be allowed one extra minute to talk with the other teams in your cluster to see if you can arrive at a strategy for all. After you are done conferring with your cluster, you will have a minute to discuss with your partner before you write down your selection. Remember, don't write down your selection until after you have had a chance to talk with your partner alone. (Note a simple strategy for the bonus rounds is for the cluster to agree to mark all Bs, thus gaining a $20 bonus. However, even after agreeing to this, one or more team may decide to go behind the back of the others and mark an A, thus gaining the bigger prize!) Keep your own money totals on your tally sheet.

6. Ask if there are any questions. If not, begin the game following these steps:
    - allow one minute for teams to confer (for bonus rounds 4, 6, and 8 allow a minute for clusters to confer followed by a minute for teams to confer);
    - after the teams confer, ask for choices to be circled (when done, pens down!);
    - have adults serve as judges and verify choices;
    - refer each team to the board to determine their pay-off;
    - have each team keep their own tally.

7. After completing eight rounds, award the winning teams in each cluster with a prize (holy card, piece of candy, round of applause). Have the clusters arrange themselves so that they can all see and hear you for the next part of the presentation.

Part I: No Shortcuts Here!

(about 50 minutes)

1. Begin the lesson with a reference to the game in the Opening Activity. Say:

   > The worldly game of life is like the game we just played. It's filled with a search for the big pay-off. People want to get into the best colleges in order to get the best jobs in order to live in the best houses in order to drive the best cars in order to take the best vacations. People want to change the color of their hair, lose weight, and remove wrinkles in order to look younger and better. People want pills that will take away the pain *now*, and not a moment later. In fact, in pursuit of the big pay-off, people try several shortcuts. There are fast-foods and diet pills and college correspondence classes that offer degrees in a fraction of the time of other schools. There are lottery games and drive-through banking, lots of things designed to shorten the process of achieving the big pay-off. (Ask the participants to share a strategy from the game they just played for immediately being awarded the big pay-off; that is, choosing all As in the hope that the other teams would all choose Bs.)

2. Distribute some popular magazines and scissors to each cluster. Ask the participants to search for photos or advertisements (i.e., products that promise quick results with little work) that represent the "shortcut" mentality. Each person should cut out one photo or advertisement of this kind. While the groups are working, pass around the poster board cross and glue stick and have each person glue his or her clipping to the cross in collage form. Allow about five to ten minutes.

3. Ask the groups to clean their areas. Collect the magazines and scissors. Then, compare taking a shortcut in order to achieve a goal to the real sacrifices and commitments people must take in order to (write on board):

   - **run a first marathon**
   - **achieve straight A's**
   - **become a great musician**
   - **be a good and loyal friend**

   Call on volunteers to list some of the sacrifices and commitments that go with each. Then, ask: "What are some sacrifices and commitments that go with being a follower of Jesus?" Allow a few responses (i.e., going to Mass, loving our neighbor, giving money to the poor). Interrupt the discussion and place a crucifix before the group. Say:

   > If we are following Jesus, this is where we are headed . . . to the cross. Look closely at this crucifix. Some of you may wear one around your neck on a chain. Actually, the crucifix is a piece of wood with a man nailed to it. Imagine if Jesus had come in the twentieth century and was executed in the electric chair. Would Christians then have a figure of a dead man strapped in an electric chair hanging on the walls of their churches and homes? Well, the cross is no different. It's the sign of a violent and cruel death, even more so because Jesus was an innocent man who had committed no crime. As you watch the following video clip, think a

bit more about the sacrifices and commitments involved in being a follower of a man who faced this kind of death.

4. Start the *Jesus of Nazareth* video at the place where Jesus is being scourged by the Roman soldiers. Play through to his last words on the cross (about twelve minutes). After the video, say:

> We are surrounded by promises and guarantees of short cuts, quick fixes, low cost, no cost, no pain, no commitment, and no obligation. In return, we are offered everything we ever dreamed of. On the other hand, Jesus offers us no short cuts in order to gain new life. He says that in order to have new life, we must die. There is no running away from the cross if we decide we want to follow Jesus. Saint John Vianney put it this way (refer the participants to page 55 in the Participant Book):
>
> "We must never lose sight of the fact that we are either saints or outcasts, that we must live for heaven or for hell: there is no middle path in this. You either belong wholly to the world or wholly to God."
>
> That isn't to say that we don't have doubts about accepting the challenge to give up our life in order to follow. In fact, the first disciples—later to become great saints—had many doubts themselves when challenged by Jesus.

Exercise

5. Ask the participants to take a bible, a pen, and book and move to a table with their cluster group from the Opening Activity. Tell them to turn to page 56, "Call to Discipleship." Read the directions and work through Part I with the group (Jesus said that he would be handed over to the Gentiles, suffer, be killed, and rise three days later). Then assign the participants to work on Parts II and III (with their clusters) and Part IV (on their own). Tell them they will be asked to share with their cluster group their answers to the Part IV question.

6. Allow about ten to twelve minutes for the students to work on the exercise. Go over the answers to parts II and III.

   ### Answers
   Part II: The disciples reacted with indignation and misunderstanding: Peter argued with Jesus about accepting such a fate: the other disciples discussed plans for greatness.

   Part III: Jesus said that he expects his disciples to pick up their cross and follow, to be the last of all and the servant of all.

7. Say:

> Share your answer to the Part IV question with your cluster group. Remember to offer a specific plan of action for your decision to follow Jesus. The person with the neatest handwriting can go first.

8. After everyone has shared, dismiss the participants for a short break. Tell them to return to the area you have reserved for the Prayer Experience after the break. They will need a pen and their books.

Break

(about 5 minutes)

Allow a brief time for a stretch, drink of water, etc. During the break, ask one of the adults to help set up for the Prayer Experience. Place a candle, a bowl of holy water, the poster cross with collage, and the crucifix in the center of the room. Have the tape or CD player cued with reflective music. If possible, arrange the chairs in a circle. If not, have the group sit on the floor around the center items. Also, plan to personally greet the guest speaker you have arranged to speak on conversion. Plan to have the speaker join the group as part of the circle and give his or her presentation at the start of the Prayer Experience.

Prayer Experience: Dying and Rising

(about 35 minutes)

Presentation

1. After the group is seated, introduce the guest speaker (see Special Preparation, page 84). Allow twenty minutes for the speaker(s) to share personal experiences of dying and rising. If time permits, allow for questions. (Thank the speaker after the presentation. Extend an invitation to the speaker to stay for the remainder of the Prayer Experience but allow option to leave.)

2. Introduce the rest of the Prayer Experience, attempting to tie-in the speaker's message. Say:

> Anything worthwhile—be it running a marathon, being a good musician, or achieving good grades—requires commitment and sacrifice. Achieving new goals also means leaving old ways behind. An athlete gives up junk food for a balanced diet. A student interested in getting better grades gives up hours of social activities to study. Look at the collage of items on the cross. How many of these would you need to personally give up in order to be a better follower of Jesus? Each of us can list several examples of ways that we have grown and moved forward by leaving old ways behind. Let's take a few minutes to look more closely at some of these times.

3. Tell the participants to open their books to page 57, "My, How I've Changed!" Allow about five minutes for them to reflect on the quotation from Saint Paul and jot notes for each of the three questions. Play the reflective music while the participants work quietly in a spirit of prayer. Conclude the time by reading Ephesians 2:1-10 (the generosity of God's plan) to the group. Then, say:

> Share your reflections from pages 57-58 with a person sitting on either side of you.

Jesus, Should I Follow You?

4. Call an end to the sharing by reading from Paul's letter to the Philippians 3:7-16 (I keep my attention on the finish line). Then say:

> When you were baptized, the minister poured water on you three times symbolizing the three days that Jesus spent in the tomb. After the baptism he said: "You have become a new creation, and have clothed yourself in Christ." To remind us of our call from death to new life, I invite you to come, one at a time, to the bowl of holy water and symbolically wash your hands in the bowl as a symbol of washing away your old self and making space for a new life. As you do, say what part of your life you ask Jesus to help you change; for example, "I ask Jesus to help me wash away my bad habit of using foul language." I will go first. Anyone may go next.

5. Allow time for all to participate. If possible, play quiet music throughout. When everyone has finished, join hands and pray the Our Father.

Part II:
Signs of New Life, Signed with New Life

(about 30 minutes)

1. For the final part of the session, make sure the participants have their books and a pen handy. They can remain in the prayer area.

2. After everyone is reassembled, call on volunteers to comment on what it would feel like to:
   - practice for a baseball season and have every game rained out;
   - write a twenty-page research report for a class and never receive it back;
   - work all day at a fast-food restaurant and not get paid.

3. Summarize the discussion. Say:

> Part of the reward of any work we do is the work itself. The struggle to improve and be the best we can be is rewarding. But, as people, we look for other rewards—pay-offs—for our efforts. A baseball player wants to play in a game. A student who writes a report wants a grade from the teacher. A worker wants to get paid. Similarly, those who choose to "lose their life" and accept Jesus' call to the cross do so in the hope of rising from death to life. For Christians, believing in the resurrection—and living the resurrection—is central to our faith. In fact, without belief in Jesus' resurrection and our share in it, our faith, according to Saint Paul, is empty. He wrote: (read 1 Cor 15:13-19, 29-32).

4. Turn on the fan full blast and blow it in the direction of the participants. Move it around so that everyone gets a good blast! Then, ask, "What do you feel?" Keep asking until someone uses the word "wind." Continue:

> How do you know it's wind? You cannot see the wind. How do you know it's there? The bottom line is that you cannot see wind, but you can see its effects. You see papers shuffled, dust scattered, hair messed up. There is a saying that goes "seeing is believing." Yet, wind is an example of something that we cannot directly

see but that we believe exists. In essence, we work backward: we see the effects of wind and arrive at the conclusion that there is wind. The same is true when it comes to believing in the existence of the Risen Jesus and in everlasting life.

We cannot see the Risen Jesus walking around in the flesh as the first disciples did, but we can see some dramatic evidence of his presence. When we see people who are willing to accept all forms of suffering, persecution, trials, and despair in the hope of sharing in the resurrection of the Risen Jesus, these are powerful signs of hope. These are powerful signs that the Risen Jesus does indeed live in them.

A few minutes ago during the Prayer Experience you asked Jesus to fill you with new life as part of your old life was washed away. Your words and actions were in themselves evidence of the presence of the Risen Jesus. True, there are no shortcuts to the resurrection and eternal life. When we commit to following Jesus, we commit to a life of sacrifice. But when we allow ourselves to die to sin, we are filled with new life. And we become signs of that new life for others!

We will be moving to our "alone" spots to reflect on some of what we believe about the resurrection and new life. (When all are in their quiet areas, ask them to turn to pages 59-60, "Life After Life," and write their responses to each of the three entries.)

Journal Activity

5. Allow about fifteen minutes for writing. Call the group back to the large group area and ask several participants to share their reflections to any one of the three questions. Continue until you have heard a representative amount of responses to each question.

Conclusion

(about 5 minutes)

Mentor Meeting Reminder

1. Remind the participants of Teen-Mentor Meeting 6. Make sure they record any specific information or directions concerning the meeting in the Mentor Memo panel.
2. Tell the participants the date and time of the next session. Dismiss them on time.

session Seven

Jesus, Are You With Me Now?

Objectives

The purpose of this session is to help the participants:
- understand different meanings of presence and become more aware of the ways the Risen Jesus is present to us;
- explore how Jesus' presence is highlighted and "crystallized" in the ritual celebration of eucharist;
- identify how rituals and meals are two ways people heighten presence.

Overview

Various aspects of *presence* are explored at this session to help the participants explore the ways that Jesus is truly present in the church. The opening activity helps the participants understand their own key roles as church, the Body of Christ. In Part I, they learn to differentiate between personal and physical presence. The significance of Jesus' meal ministry and the common experience of sharing traditional meals with family and friends is compared. In Part II this lesson—the roles that storytelling, meals, and ritual play in recalling a past experience or person—is looked at in more detail. Finally, the participants focus on the eucharist as the ritual meal the church celebrates in experiencing the real presence of Jesus.

Mentor Component

Preview Teen-Mentor Meeting 7. Provide help as needed for one or more of the Activity Suggestoins.

Session Outline

Opening Activity: In Search of the Church (about 20 minutes)
Part I: Close Encounters: Understanding Presence (about 55 minutes)
Break (about 5 minutes)
Part II: Same As It Ever Was . . . (about 40 minutes)
Prayer Experience: In the Breaking of the Bread (about 20 minutes)
Conclusion (about 10 minutes)

Supplies

For this session you will need:
- four index cards with scavenger hunt clues
- four 8 1/2" x 11" pieces of paper with one letter (C, H, C, or H) printed on each
- masking tape
- candle
- tape or CD player
- (optional) recording of "haunted house" sounds
- bibles (New Testaments) for each participant
- pens
- video of *How the Grinch Stole Christmas*
- VCR and monitor
- a birthday cake, candles, matches, paper plates, plastic forks, napkins
- a communion plate with consecrated hosts, a table prepared with a cloth, and two candles for the Prayer Experience
- recording of "Jesus, the Bread of Life" (Grayson Warren Brown from the album *Hymns of a Soulful People*)
- bible marked to the following passages: Lk 22:14-19 and Lk 24:13-35

Special Preparations

1. A scavenger hunt is part of the opening activity. You will need four clues (each written on an index card) to direct groups of participants to different areas of your locale. If you are meeting at a church, you might consider using these clues and locations:

Clue	Location
A place where brides and fathers begin their final twenty yards together	Main door of the church
A resting place for birds and the patron of our church	Outdoor statue of patron saint
If Father had a Mercedes he'd park it here.	Pastor's parking space
Barney, Ernie, and Big Bird live here	Nursery room

You will need to place one 8 1/2" x 11" piece of paper (with the letters C, H, C, or H) at each location.
2. In Part II the birthday cake is used as a lead-in for a discussion about ritual. Find out the name of the person with the closest birthday to the date of the session.
3. (optional) In lieu of the Prayer Experience, offer a eucharistic celebration. Arrange for a priest to celebrate with the group. Brief him beforehand on the session's main objectives.

Setting

You will need the following areas for this session:
1. A large group area where you can gather the groups in a relaxed and informal atmosphere. There should be viewing access to a board or easel.
2. An area where the participants can meet around tables. This area should also be suitable for a "birthday party" (for eating cake, drinking punch, etc.).
3. An area for the Prayer Experience. Adapt the large group area into a comfortable setting for prayer with a table, covered with cloth and with two candles, in the center.

Note: It is recommended that this session be held in the evening so that you can take advantage of the effect darkness has on our understanding of physical and personal presence.

Opening Activity: In Search of the Church

(about 20 minutes)

1. Welcome the participants as they arrive. Ask them to check in with their group moderators and show their Teen-Mentor Meeting 6 summary sheet and verification signature. After check-in, the participants should bring their books and pens and move to the large group area.
2. Have the participants count off to four groups. Assign each group an adult leader. Have all the participants sit down while you explain the directions for the following game.

Scavenger Hunt

3. Say:

> You are going on a scavenger hunt (on the church grounds). You'll be staying together with your group leader. Leader, raise your hand. The easy thing about the scavenger hunt is that your group will only be given one clue. You'll only have to find one item. The more difficult part of the game is that you'll have to use all the items collected by all the groups to solve a puzzle. After your group has found your item, return to this room and we will continue with the game.

4. Distribute one index card with a clue written on it to each group leader. Tell each group to huddle with their leader to solve the clue and then to go together to the location to see if they were correct and they can locate the item. Remind all the

participants to stay with their leaders. Allow about five minutes for everyone to return. (If a group is having difficulty, send a runner out to provide them with an extra hint.) Collect the "items" (the papers with C, H, C, or H written on them) as the groups return. Tape them on the board in the order they were given to you but leave two spaces in between the first two letters and the last two letters (i.e., H C _ _ C H). When everyone has returned, and is seated, say:

> You've done a good job with the first part of this game. You've found the right items, the letters here on the board. Now your task is to arrange the letters to form a word. Clue: the word has something to do with what we are going to talk about tonight.

5. After a couple of unusual guesses, someone will likely point out the word is "church," but that it's missing two letters. Say:

> You are right. You are the heart and center of church. (Rearrange the letters on the board and write "U" and "R" in the center.) You've just spent some time moving with your group to various locations around the church property. (Ask a volunteer in each group to share the clue they were given and its solution.) If someone asked you to point to the church, you might choose one of these locations or the church building itself. It might take you quite a bit of time to recognize that indeed, you are the church! Similarly, if someone asked you to point out Jesus' presence in the church, where would you point? As Catholics, we believe Jesus is really present with us on our earthly journey. If he's really present, where is he? How do we see him? Let's look at some different ways.

Part I:
Close Encounters: Understanding Presence

(about 55 minutes)

1. Darken the room (or move to a separate room that is already darkened). The darker the room the better! Have the participants sit on the floor. Light one candle and place it near you on the floor. To add to the eerie feeling, play a tape of haunted house sounds in the background (optional). Prepare to speak from the following script.

Script

> 2. There's something about sitting in the dark that's creepy. As kids, I'm sure most of you sat around at camp or at a sleep-over and told ghost stories. Even in your home you probably had occasions when the darkness of your own bedroom overwhelmed you. You may have felt certain that someone or something was lurking near your bed ready to grab you. Darkness plays tricks on us. In the dark, we don't see with our eyes. Instead, we try to "see" with our other senses. We try to sense how far away someone is, what position they're in, whether or not they're moving or still. Though we can't see through the darkness, we are acutely aware of the presence of another.

> Presence is a strange thing. There are really two kinds of presence. The kind we are most familiar with is physical presence. Each of us is physically present to the other in this room right now. However, someone can be present to us even if they are not physically with us. We call this personal presence. We can sometimes be so aware of a person that we feel that person's presence, even though he or she may not be right with us at the moment. For example, what if, as the lights are out, one of you had the idea that you'll sneak out of the session, leave the premises, and go down to the corner market for a soda and candy bar? What's stopping you? Well, for some people it may be their mom's disappointment after she's been told what you've done: "I can't believe you did that," she would say. "You've really disappointed me." For another, it might be your father's angry words that you hear: "You're grounded this weekend," he might say. Though your parents aren't physically here, you definitely feel their personal presence.
>
> Personal presence doesn't only have to do with the corrective voice of an adult. Someone may feel the presence of a classmate who is absent from school for the day. A couple in love may feel the personal presence of the other even when separated. A husband whose wife had died commented that he could "feel her presence" at certain times of the day ("like morning when we used to share a cup of coffee together") and in certain places ("her closet still smells of her fragrance"). And Christians often describe occasions when Jesus is present with them. How do you understand personal presence?

Journal Activity

3. Turn on the lights in the room. Ask the participants to open their books to page 63. Read or paraphrase the introductory paragraph. Then allow ten to fifteen minutes for the participants to read the story, "Hank Lives," and complete the journal activity that follows on page 65, "Understanding Presence."

Discussion Follow-up

4. Ask the participants to pair with a partner and share what they wrote in the Journal Activity. Allow about five minutes. Then, call time and ask volunteers to share some ways people can feel the presence of another even though the person is not physically present to them. List these ways on the board, for example:
    - doing an activity you once shared with the person
    - recalling the person's words and actions
    - hearing the person's favorite song
    - eating the person's favorite food

   Continue with the lesson script, explaining another example of presence.

Script (continued)

> 5. Imagine you were a student at Loyola Marymount. You were at the game when Bo Kimble shot the left-handed free-throw. Now, it's many years later. You've been invited back to school for a reunion. You get there early and go into the gym. You

see the spot where Hank Gathers collapsed. You seem to hear the hush of the crowd that accompanied that moment. You also remember Bo Kimble's free-throw and the wild enthusiasm and emotion that accompanied that game. The entire experience comes back to you. Later, at the reunion, you retell the stories over dinner. There are people at your table who graduated ten, twenty, and even fifty years ago. Yet the experience of Hank and Bo and you becomes present to everyone at the table as you share a meal together. The past becomes present.

In much the same way, Jesus' disciples had a profound experience that changed their lives forever. The Risen Jesus appeared to them on several occasions. He was a man they had seen put to death yet who continued to be physically present to them. He told them: "Look at my hands and my feet, that it is I myself. Touch me and see, because a ghost does not have flesh and bones as you can see I have" (Lk 24:39). Then, as they got used to this presence, Jesus was taken from them again, when he ascended to heaven. How would they experience his presence now? The disciples recalled Jesus' words to them at the Last Supper. (Read Lk 22:14-19.)

Jesus knew that one of the best and most common ways that people experience the presence of one another is by sharing a meal together. As in the story of the college reunion, when we share a meal with others, we are present to others. As we tell stories over a meal, the past becomes present to us as well. Food, stories, and presence go hand in hand. Let's examine this technique a little more.

Small Group Exercise

6. Ask the participants to gather with their small groups from the Opening Activity. Tell the participants to open their books to page 66, "Invited to the Lord's Table." Distribute bibles, and assign each group ten minutes to complete the scripture exercise.

7. Say:

   The exercise on page 66 briefly describes several of the meals Jesus shared with people. When Jesus ate with people he used the occasion to become more a part of their lives. How? For example:

   - Jesus went to their homes.
   - Jesus appreciated hospitality.
   - Jesus enjoyed socializing.
   - Jesus was comfortable with men, women, and children.
   - Jesus was concerned with the physical and spiritual well being of all.

   Can you recognize some of the same elements from Jesus' meals in the meals you share with others? Look over the list of meal occasions at the bottom of page 67. Choose one meal to talk about with your group. Tell about things like the time and place of the meal, something you learned, the food you ate, and why the meal was meaningful to you. The person who lives the closest to a McDonald's goes first.

8. Allow ten to twelve minutes for everyone to share. Then, say:

> We've looked at how people can be present to one another and how meals and telling stories over meals can heighten that presence. After a short break, we'll take a closer look at how Jesus is present with us in a special meal called eucharist.

Break

(about 5 minutes)

Allow a brief time for a stretch and drink of water. Do not allow other forms of drink in observance of the one hour communion fast. Tell the participants to meet back in the large group area after the break. During the break prepare the birthday cake with candles for the "surprise" that is to follow. Also, make sure the *How the Grinch Stole Christmas* video is cued and ready to be shown.

Part II: Same As It Ever Was . . .

(about 40 minutes)

1. After the group has returned to the large group area, light the candles on the birthday cake, darken the lights in the room, and bring the cake into the room while singing "Happy Birthday" to the participant whose birthday is closest to the date of this session. After the song, tell the participants that they will enjoy the cake a little later. Continue with a lesson on rituals. Say:

> We just experienced something called a ritual. What is a definition of ritual? (Allow the participants to suggest definitions; fill in as necessary: A ritual is a habitual way of doing something to express or commemorate a significant experience.) The birthday ritual is one ritual we are familiar with. Let's expand on it some more. If we were going to really celebrate N's birthday with a full-blown celebration, what other things would we include as part of the ritual?

2. List the suggestions on the board and discuss. The list might include, for example:
   - lights out
   - element of surprise
   - singing "Happy Birthday"
   - cake
   - making a wish
   - blowing out candles
   - wearing party hats
   - decorations and balloons
   - opening presents
   - reading birthday cards
   - playing games
   - eating cake and ice cream

Session Seven

3. Continue the discussion. Ask questions like the following:
   - What does the birthday ritual express or accomplish?
   - Why do we celebrate birthdays of people who are no longer physically present like Abraham Lincoln, Martin Luther King, and Jesus? (Focus on how that person's continued presence is heightened by marking the date of his or her birth with a ritual celebration.)
   - What are some other rituals associated with holidays or celebrations? (New Year's Eve, Thanksgiving, trick-or-treating, etc.)
   - How do you think rituals begin?
4. Allow some time for the participants to suggest how rituals begin. Then present an explanation based on the following script.

Script

5. It's really easy to see how rituals begin. For example, imagine that the following incident happened to you:

    You and all of your best friends attended a youth retreat together and had the most exceptional experience possible. All of you were overwhelmed. You never felt closer to your friends or to God in all your life.

    On the way home from the retreat, you continue to feel this closeness with one another. You're laughing and joking and telling stories. You stop off to get some pizza. At the restaurant the storytelling and laughing and fun go on. You even get the waitress to laugh and joke with your group. It feels like the whole world is part of your party. The good times continue on the ride home. As you are all dropped off at home, everyone hugs and says an emotional good-bye.

    The next time you meet you talk about what a great time you all had, especially over pizza. You're all eager to have that kind of fun again. You try to recreate the experience as well as you can:
    - You refer to the whole idea as "our pizza thing" (i.e., "Let's do our pizza thing this Friday night!").
    - You go to the same restaurant that you call "the place."
    - You request the same table and waitress. Everyone sits in the same chair.
    - You order the same number of pizzas with the same toppings as always.
    - You share some of the same stories and jokes you did before and you remember some of what happened on the retreat.
    - You leave in the same manner with hugs and farewells.

    Do you see what happened here? You've begun a ritual. In this case, a ritual meal. In an attempt to make the past experience present, you try to recreate the event through stories and actions that recall the initial experience. Rituals recapture the past, bring it into the present, and make it real again.

    Let's look at another example of how rituals makes things present to us.

6. Show a segment of *How the Grinch Stole Christmas* focusing on how the Grinch tries to steal the celebration by stealing the ritual. Show about ten minutes of the video just to refresh the memories of the participants (99 percent will have seen it dozens of times).

7. After the video clip, ask:

- What was the Grinch trying to do?
- What was the Who's ritual for celebrating Christmas?
- What happened after the Grinch stole the Who's ritual?
- What does this story teach us about ritual?

Then, continue with the script.

Script (continued)

8. If your birthday came and no one celebrated the ritual, would it still be your birthday? Of course. But the ritual makes your birthday—and the uniquely special person it celebrates—more real, more present to you and to all. If New Year's Eve passed and no one celebrated the New Year's Eve ritual, would it still be New Year's? Of course. But the lighting of fireworks, the sound of party favors, the hugs and kisses, and the singing of "Auld Lang Syne" make the passing of the old year and the arrival of the new year more real . . . more present. In celebrating such rituals, we become more present to one another as well.

    The Grinch tried to steal the presence of Christmas by stealing the ritual and found that it couldn't be done. Christmas was present anyway . . . the ritual was just a way of making the experience more present.

    As Catholic Christians, we have been taught to believe that Jesus is present with us at all times. Most of you probably understand and accept this to one degree or another. But, being the humans that we are, we need reminders, signs, symbols, and rituals to heighten his presence. The eucharist is the prime ritual given to us by Jesus to celebrate his presence. If the Grinch tried to burn down all the churches in the world and steal all the things we need to celebrate the eucharist, would Jesus still be present? Would the church still exist? Yes! But the place we gather on Sundays and the ritual meal we celebrate are meant to make his presence more real to us.

    A few minutes ago we looked at the birthday ritual and listed all of the ingredients that go into it. Now, let's take a look at the ritual of the eucharist to see how Jesus' presence is made more real for us.

9. Tell the participants to turn to page 68, "The Ritual of the Eucharist." Ask them to work with a partner and brainstorm actions, objects, and words that are repeated the same way over and over at Mass. Explain that they can write their notes anywhere on the page and that they will be asked to share their list with the entire group. Allow a few minutes, then list some of the things (i.e. procession to santuary, altar, candles, songs, "The Lord Be with You," "Alleluia," "Amen," etc.) on the board. Emphasize things that are always constant. Relate the notion of "sameness" to the elements in the pizza story. Also, discuss one or more of the following:

- the value of the eucharistic rituals;
- how some of the necessary "sameness" of ritual at Mass is often perceived as boring by teens;
- how the ritual heightens Jesus' presence.

Then, prepare the participants to move to the area for the Prayer Experience.

Prayer Experience: In the Breaking of the Bread

(about 20 minutes)

1. Gather the group in the area you have reserved for prayer. To begin, dim the lights and light the candles. Place the communion plate with the consecrated hosts on the table. Say:

   > Jesus is always present with us. He is with us when we go to school, spend time with our friends, play sports, learn a new skill. But when we gather with our Christian community around the altar—especially in Sunday liturgy—we celebrate a ritual that is removed from the normal bounds of time and space. We celebrate Jesus' real presence, so real that we, as believers, are with Jesus the same way that the first disciples were at the Last Supper. Over the years, several actions, objects, and words have developed into a ritual of that occasion first shared with the apostles on the night before Jesus died. Primarily, Jesus is present in the breaking of the bread and the sharing of the cup. Even those who first walked with Jesus had a hard time recognizing how this was so.

2. Call on a good reader to read the Emmaus story (Lk 24:13-35) to the group. Then, discuss one or more of the following points with the group:
   - how the two travellers were restrained from recognizing Jesus;
   - how Jesus listened to their story and then told them his story;
   - how they recognized Jesus the instant he broke bread with them;
   - the differences and similarities between Jesus' physical and personal appearance in the story.

3. Conclude the discussion. Say:

   > At eucharist, the church celebrates a ritual meal with bread and wine that clearly reveals Jesus' presence. The appearance of the bread is, in itself, quite ordinary. It looks and tastes like regular bread. But it is much more than that. When we celebrate a ritual using the bread, hear the words that Jesus spoke, and are led by a person ordained to lead us, the reality of the event changes. Jesus is truly present with us in the breaking of the bread, the sharing of the cup, the proclamation of his word, the lives of the people gathered. Our awareness of Jesus' presence, is heightened dramatically at the celebration of this special ritual meal.

4. Ask the group to prepare to receive communion. Recite the Our Father together. Then, say:

   > As you receive the bread of life, hold it in your hand until everyone is ready to share (demonstrate).

Distribute communion in the hand. Say, "Body of Christ." (Response: Amen.) Continue:

> This is Jesus, the Lamb of God, who takes away the sins of the world. Happy are those who are called to his supper. (Response: Lord, I am not worthy to receive you, but only say the word and I shall be healed.)
>
> May the Body of Christ bring us to everlasting life. (Response: Amen.)

5. Lead the group in receiving communion. Start the recording of "Jesus, the Bread of Life" (Grayson Warren Brown, *Hymns of a Soulful People*). Motion the group to sit on the floor. When the song ends, sit quietly for a minute or two in silence. Then conclude:

> Since we recognize Jesus' presence in ourselves and in one another, let us offer a sign of peace to one another as we go on our way in love and service of the Lord. (Lead a sharing of a sign of peace.)

Conclusion

(about 10 minutes)

Mentor Meeting Reminder

1. Remind the participants of Teen-Mentor Meeting 7. Make sure they record any specific information or directions concerning the meeting in the Mentor Memo panel.
2. Ask the participants to move back to the room with tables. Pass out paper plates, napkins, forks, and a piece of the birthday cake to each person. Celebrate!

Jesus, Am I Ready to Follow You?

session Eight

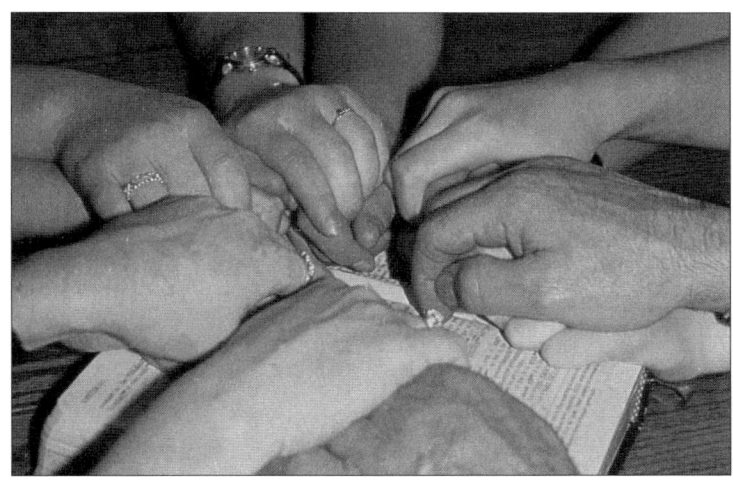

Objectives

The purpose of this session is to help the participants:
- come to a better understanding of what Jesus invites them to when he offers us "fullness of life" and of the risks that go with accepting the invitation;
- consider their own readiness to follow Jesus and the fears and obstacles that stand in the way;
- receive encouragement and affirmation to deepen their commitments to follow Jesus.

Overview

Jesus said, "I came so that you might have life and have it more abundantly" (Jn 10:10). This offer of fullness of life is the reward of discipleship. In this final session the participants explore Jesus' understanding of completeness as doing the Father's will and consider the degree to which they are willing to take the risks that go along with Christian discipleship. After naming fears and obstacles that prevent them from following Jesus, the participants reflect personally on their readiness to make a commitment to Jesus. In this last session of the course, there is also a great deal of opportunity for the teens and adults alike to provide affirmation to one another as they continue in the challenge to be better Christians.

Mentor Component

The teens and mentors are to meet for a final time at this session. Provide space for the teens and mentors to confer on their own and to conduct the meeting as suggested in Teen-Mentor Meeting 8 pages 76-77.

Session Outline

Opening Activity: Guts (about 20 minutes)

Part I: The Really Good Life (about 40 minutes)

Break (about 5 minutes)

Part II: Getting in the Boat, Storm-Filled Waters (about 30 minutes)

Prayer Experience: Do Not Be Afraid (about 20 minutes)

Mentor Meeting (Reception) and Conclusion (about 35 minutes)

Supplies

For this session you will need:
- one deck of playing cards (each with a different back or design) per every six participants
- blindfolds (torn strips of fabric will do)
- small plates or bowls
- a variety of unusual foods in texture and taste (i.e., gummy worm candies, peaches, sauerkraut, pudding, walnuts, kiwi).
- prizes (i.e., movie passes) for the winners of the game
- video of *Star Wars: Return of the Jedi* set at the point where Luke is training to be a Jedi knight under the watchful eye of his mentor Yoda
- VCR and monitor
- five posters (8 1/2" x 11") marked: Definitely True, Usually True, Somewhat/Sometimes True, Seldom True, Never True
- masking tape
- slips of paper (1" x 2")
- hat
- tape or CD player and recording of "All That Is Hidden" (Bernadette Farrell, OCP Publications) or another song with lyrics that speak of the challenges and rewards of discipleship
- a stack of feedback slips (3" x 5" pieces of paper)
- bible marked to the following passages: Mk 1:16-20; Mt 9:27-31; Mt 9:9; Lk 4:16-30; Lk 12:16-21

Special Preparations

1. Adapt the conclusion of the session to the special character of your course. Invite the mentors as far in advance as possible. For any participants whose mentors cannot be present, invite a parent or other significant adult to be with them at this occasion. Specify the time for arrival. Invite two or three teens to share reflections on the mentor experience (see page 112, No.2).
2. Arrange for hospitality items as you desire.

Setting

You will need the following areas for this session:
1. A large group area where you can gather the groups in a relaxed and informal atmosphere. There should be viewing access to a chalkboard or easel.
2. An area where the participants can meet around tables.
3. An area for the Prayer Experience. The floor of the church sanctuary often works well. If this area is impossible to use, arrange the large group area into a comfortable setting for prayer.
4. "Alone" areas where the teens and mentors can meet apart from the rest of the group.
5. (optional) An area for serving and enjoying food and drink.

Opening Activity: Guts

(about 20 minutes)

1. Welcome the participants as they arrive. Ask them to check in with their group moderators and show their Teen-Mentor Meeting 7 summary sheet and verification signature, if due. After check-in, the participants should bring their book and a pen and move to the area with small group tables.
2. Randomly distribute one playing card (an equal amount from each deck that you will use to form groups of six people) to each participant. Place the remaining cards of each deck face down at separate tables. Ask the participants to take a seat at a table with the deck that corresponds to their card.

Game

3. Assign a "dealer" at each table. (A criterion might be the ability to shuffle cards!) Explain the game in the following manner. Say:

> There is a kid's television show called *Guts* but let me tell you that the game we are about to play makes the TV show version look like kindergarten stuff in comparison. We're going to see who has really got some guts in this group . . . who's really willing to take some risks.
>
> You already have one card. Place it face up in front of you. Your dealer will then deal you two other cards. Keep those two cards face down. Do not let anyone else see your face-down cards.
>
> Beginning with the player at the dealer's left, you will have a chance to decide if you have the "best" hand in the group. For our purposes, the best hand means high cards (go over the point values as necessary: ace=11, face cards=10, etc.). Remember, all you can go on is the one card you see in front of each player and your own cards.
>
> If you think your hand has a chance of winning, say, "I've got guts!" If you don't think you have a chance to win say, "I'm wimping out." No matter what, do not show your cards until everyone in your group has a chance to declare his or her intentions.

Jesus, Should I Follow You?

> The person in each group with the highest hand will receive a prize. (Announce the prize. Make the prize enticing enough to encourage the participants to take a risk.) Those who "wimp out" will have to pay the price by doing some kind of cleanup work when the game is over. Those who stayed in but lost to the highest hand will suffer a more severe penalty that I can't tell you about yet.
>
> Any questions? (Pause to answer.) Let's play "Guts"!

4. Instruct the dealers to distribute two cards, face down, to each player (including himself or herself). Then:
   - Ask the player at the dealer's left to declare either "I've got guts" or "I'm wimping out." Continue around the table. The dealer declares last. (Remember, no one reveals his or her cards until everyone has declared.)
   - Have all those who "wimped out" move to the other side of the room.
   - Have those still playing reveal their hidden cards one player at a time beginning with the player at the dealer's left to determine who has the highest hand. (In the case of a tie, have the participants each draw one card from the top of the pile. The higher card is the winner.)
   - Award the winner of each group.
5. Address those who challenged but lost. Say:

   > You had enough guts to give it a try. Now, we'll see who really has guts in this group. You have your choice of the following: (1) You can take the easy way out and simply get up in front of the group and demonstrate some unique or hidden talent you have (i.e., doing a handstand, speaking a foreign language, reciting a poem, etc.); (2) If you really have guts you can prove it by moving on to the final test.

6. Allow those who choose option 1 to perform their hidden talents before the group.
7. Finally, lead any participant(s) who chose option 2 to a table and blindfold them. Tell them that you are going to place a bowl or plate in front of them with a food item that they will have to pick up with their hands and then eat. Place foods in front of them that are edible but feel gross (i.e., gummy worm candies, peaches, sauerkraut, pudding, walnuts, kiwi). Encourage the spectators to make noises suggesting that what the participant is about to eat is something gross.
8. Lead a round of applause to the participant(s) who showed such guts. Have those who first "wimped out" in the card game clean up the area and bring bibles and pens to each table.

   Optional: If the "Guts" game is not feasible, lead a "missing piece" activity. Leave a few completed puzzles (little kid puzzles will do) in the front of the room with one piece missing from each. Hide the missing pieces in the room. Allow a few minutes for the entire group to search for the missing pieces and complete the puzzles. Use many "decoy" pieces to complicate matters. Offer prizes to those who successfully complete the puzzles. Refer to the activity at the conclusion of Part I when discussing the completeness of life offered by Jesus.

Part I: The Really Good Life

(about 40 minutes)

1. Ask the participants to gather at their same small group tables and turn to page 71 in their books. Introduce the session. Ask the participants to read the introductory material. Then, say:

   > In this course, you've heard a case for Christian discipleship. You've learned that being a follower of Jesus has its rewards (i.e., truthful teachings, often miraculous actions, having a friend who remains present to you, eternal life). You've also become more aware of the challenges of following Jesus (i.e., to drop everything, pick up your cross and follow). How convinced are you that Jesus is calling you? How willing are you to trust Jesus and follow along the way?

Exercise

2. Point out the winning lottery ticket (five million dollars) on page 72, "Lotto Cash." Ask the participants to imagine the ticket was theirs. Ask: "How would your life be different if you won five million dollars? What are some of the things you would do with five million dollars? What part of your current lifestyle would you give up?" Allow ten minutes for everyone to share their responses with their groups. The person with the most money in his or her possession goes first.

3. After the discussion, say:

   > It would be very difficult for someone to win five million dollars and not change the way he or she lived. Similarly, it was difficult for the people in the gospels who met Jesus to go on living as they did before. For example:
   >
   > - Peter and Andrew left their boat, fishing nets, and their father when Jesus called them (read Mk 1:16-20).
   > - Jesus gave sight to two blind men and warned them, "See that no one knows about this." Instead, they went throughout the land proclaiming what he had done (read Mt 9:27-31).
   > - Matthew left his tax collector's post when Jesus said to him, "Follow me" (read Mt 9:9).
   > - People in the synagogue heard Jesus proclaim that the scriptures were fulfilled in him and they tried to throw him head first over the side of a cliff (read Lk 4:16-30).
   >
   > The people in the gospels had strong reactions to Jesus that lead to life-altering changes. Following (or rejecting) Jesus does not lend itself to neutrality. Following Jesus demands total commitment, the placing of Jesus before everything else.

4. Refer the participants to the Journal Activity on page 73. Read the question "What else would you need if you possessed five million dollars?" but don't offer any more clues to how the question should be answered. Allow five minutes for the participants to write individual responses. Then, call on volunteers to share what they listed. Write some of their ideas (more money, fancier cars, good

health, happy relationships, peace on earth, etc.) on the board. Make the list as long as possible. Then, continue the presentation using the following script.

Script

5. Five million dollars or, in fact, all the money in the world, doesn't make a person's life complete. As you may recall Jesus referred to this lesson in the parable of the rich fool (read Lk 12:16-21).

   Jesus knows that in spite of all kinds of material riches many people feel that their lives are not complete. Knowing that people are searching for more, Jesus offers these promises:

   - "I came so that you might have life and have it more abundantly" (Jn 10:10).
   - "I am the vine, you are the branches. Whoever remains in me and I in him will bear much fruit, because without me you can do nothing . . . I have told you this so that my joy might be in you and your joy might be complete" (Jn 15:5, 11). (Write **complete** on the board.)

   Jesus tells us that if we belong to him our lives will be *complete*. This is a very important word. Jesus does not promise us monetary riches, health, lack of worry. Rather, he says that our lives will be complete. Jesus used this word at other important moments in his life, for example:

   - When Jesus summed up what his entire teaching was about he said, "So be perfect just as your heavenly Father is perfect" (Mt 5:48). This passage is intimidating—no one can be perfect. However, when we understand that the word Jesus used can also be translated as "complete" the whole meaning changes: Be complete as your heavenly Father is complete. How is this different? What does it mean? (Allow volunteers to comment.)
   - When Jesus died on the cross he said, "It is finished"(Jn 19:30). This word, too, can be interpreted to mean complete. Jesus is not speaking as someone who feels defeated (as in, "I'm finished . . . I'm a goner"). No, when Jesus says, "It is complete," we realize he is using the words of someone who feels they have accomplished their ultimate goal. As Jesus dies on the cross, his words indicate that he feels he has done everything he could, become everything he could be, because he has fulfilled God's will.

   The message for us is that the key to the really good life is not money, health, finding the ideal boyfriend or girlfriend, satisfying career, et al. The key to the really good life is to achieve the completeness that comes with following Jesus and thereby doing God's will!

6. Ask the participants to turn to page 74, "Jesus Success Stories," and read the quotation of St. Jerome. Ask volunteers to comment on its meaning. Then tell the participants to spend five minutes brainstorming the names of people they believe have found fullness of life by following Jesus. Next, ask them to write a wise quotation about faith in Jesus or life in general that they have heard from one of the people on their list.

7. Tell the group to share their quotation with their group and to write at least one meaningful quotation that someone has shared with them under number 3 on page 74.

Break

(about 5 minutes)

Allow a brief time for a stretch, drink of water, etc. Tell the group to meet back in the large group area after the break. During the break prepare an open space in the large group area. Post the five posters you have prepared (Definitely True, Usually True, etc.) in a direct line on the wall or set them in a direct line on the floor. Leave enough space between the areas marked by the posters for the participants to be able to gather.

Part II: Getting in the Boat, Storm-Filled Waters

(about 30 minutes)

1. As the participants reassemble, ask them to write their names on a slip of paper and place it in the hat. Ask everyone to take a seat on the floor. Say:

   > Jesus often asked his followers to "get into the boat" with him as he traveled from one side of a lake to another. Jesus traveled on fishing boats certainly more primitive than those of today. Weather patterns were less understood. A storm could creep up with little notice. The water itself was likely intimidating to those who weren't fishermen. Children of the first-century world didn't spend their summers at the YMCA taking water safety courses or swimming lessons. Yet "getting into the boat" was a very practical direction from Jesus on how to be a follower.
   >
   > Getting into the boat and following Jesus across a potentially storm-filled lake to uncharted territory is a symbol of your life—past, present, and future—as a disciple. For example:
   >
   > **Getting into the boat** (write) By virtue of your baptism and through your continued practice of the faith (including participating in this course) you have accepted—maybe at times begrudgingly—your part in the journey of faith.
   >
   > **Across a storm-filled lake** (write) Following Jesus is filled with many challenges. Christians over the centuries have been ridiculed, persecuted, and killed for their faith. You may feel that your own faith life is threatened by worldly values, friends who don't understand you, or your own lack of understanding.
   >
   > **Uncharted territory** (write) Like the first followers who got into the boat with Jesus, we move forward in great hope that our final destination will satisfy our every need by bringing us into communion with family, friends, and God.

Activity

2. Make sure that everyone has placed their name in the hat. Point out the charts and say:

   > I am going to read a statement having something to do with following Jesus. Ask yourself how true the statement is of you, and sit down in front of the poster that best shows your response. Be prepared to explain your position. After everyone is seated, I will pick one name out of the hat and ask that person to explain his or her response.

3. Choose from the following statements and add your own. Pick more than one name to respond to each question.

   Statements:
   - I am willing to talk to my friends about my faith in Jesus.
   - Being a good Christian is more important to me than being a good student, musician, athlete, etc.
   - Because I am a follower of Jesus, I refrain from destructive behavior (drugs, sex, violence).
   - I pray for my enemies and try to forgive those who harm me.
   - I am committed to attending Mass each Sunday and holy day.
   - I am willing to offer my time, talents, and money to those in need like Jesus did.
   - If I hear a friend using the name of Jesus disrespectfully, I tell him or her to stop.
   - I do not gossip and I walk away when someone else is gossiping.
   - I will not lose my faith and hope in Jesus even at times of great tragedy (sickness, death of a friend or relative).
   - Because of Jesus, I believe that life will have a good and happy ending.

Prayer Experience: Do Not Be Afraid

(about 20 minutes)

1. Move to the area you have reserved for the prayer experience, or adapt the surroundings in the large group space. Ask the participants to bring their books and open them to page 75, "Do Not Be Afraid." Say:

   > As we uncovered in the last activity, there are many obstacles to following Jesus. The lake is storm-filled and we are naturally afraid. In our own lives we are afraid of not meeting the expectations of others, afraid of losing friends, afraid of suffering, afraid of what it means to really commit to following Jesus. I am going to read a story from John's gospel. As I read, try to get inside the story. Imagine what it would have been like to be there, to be one of the disciples who decided to get into the boat.

2. Read the gospel story dramatically (from the Participant Book). Try to emphasize what it would have been like to participate in the events you are narrating. After the reading, expand on the emotions and fears represented. Use the following script as the participants follow along and mark their books in column two.

Script

3. We are going to use the scripture story to help us get in touch with our own fears so that we can move forward in our relationship with Jesus. Which part of the story best describes what is going on in your heart right now?
   - It was evening when the disciples departed. It was already dark. You may feel lost and confused about Jesus' entire message, about what Jesus is really about. Everyone seems to tell you how special and important it is to know Jesus and be his follower. You still don't seem to understand. If you are in the dark about your relationship with Jesus, circle letter a.
   - The darkness doesn't scare you. You are willing to try anything once, even things you are not completely clear about. You have a sense that Jesus' message is right and true. You have willingly entered the boat. Now the wind blows and the sea is strong. You didn't expect this! It's one thing to follow Jesus, but not to the point of danger or death. If you are afraid of pain and suffering, circle letter b.
   - Jesus walks to you on water. This fear is worse. Jesus is not someone unknown or make-believe. He is real. He is standing right in front of you. That means everything you have heard about him must be true. That means you really must do what he expects of you. You must place Jesus before everything else you hold dear. If losing your life in this fashion scares you, circle c.
   - Jesus comforts you with these words, "Do not be afraid." You want to take him into the boat. You want to bring Jesus close to you. If you are truly comforted by Jesus' words, circle letter d.

   Words—like those of Jesus—are reassuring. In order to overcome our personal fears, we too need to be reassured. We need to be affirmed and encouraged to get into the boat and journey with Jesus across the great unknown.

4. Ask the participants to note the words of affirmation in the margins of page 75. Say:

   I am going to give you a slip of paper with the name of one participant. When it is your turn, offer a sentence of affirmation for the person about how or why you feel he or she makes a good follower of Jesus. For example, "I think Susie is a good follower of Jesus because she is a ferocious defender of anyone who is picked on unfairly." Use the affirmation words on page 75 to help you form sentences.

5. Distribute the slips with names (making sure no one gets his or her own name). Call on the person at your left to begin. Continue until everyone has shared. Then, say:

   Each of us possesses many strengths, qualities, and characteristics to overcome the obstacles and fears that prevent us from following Jesus. Most importantly, however, we have Jesus himself to strengthen us.

6. Play the recording of "All That Is Hidden" or another appropriate song that speaks of the challenges and rewards of discipleship.

Mentor Meeting (Reception) and Conclusion

(about 35 minutes)

1. Assemble in a different area from where you had the prayer experience. Welcome the mentors. Ask the participants to sit with their mentors. Then, immediately play a five-minute clip from the *Star Wars: Return of the Jedi* video in which Luke Skywalker is training to become a Jedi knight under the watchful eye of his mentor Yoda. After the video clip, say:

   > We have learned quite a bit about the challenge of following Jesus. Like Luke Skywalker, we have often considered giving up because it seemed too difficult. However, just as young Luke had Yoda to teach him, our teens have been blessed with mentors as well. Throughout this mini-course they have had adults to meet with, to discuss with, and to ask questions of. We appreciate the contribution of all the adults—mentors, team members, and parents—who have participated in this course.

2. Invite two or three participants to share general reflections about the mentor relationship on behalf of all the teens. (These speakers should be invited and prepared in advance of the session.) The reflections might include some or all of the following points:
   - admiration for the example of the mentor in being a follower of Jesus;
   - appreciation for the time the mentor spent meeting with you;
   - a special lesson learned from the mentor.

   Conclude the talks with a round of applause for all the mentors.

3. Distribute letter quality paper, pens, and envelopes to each person. Ask the participants and mentors to move to "alone" spots to conduct their final meeting, Teen-Mentor Meeting 8 on pages 76-77 of the Participant Book. Tell them to follow the letter writing tips under Activity Suggestions, write a letter to their partner, seal it in an envelope, and exchange it at the end of the period.
   Note: It is imperative that everyone—teen and mentor—receives a letter. If you know of anyone who cannot attend, encourage them to write their letter and bring it to you before the session. Also, have the adult team members ready to write personal letters to teens or mentors who are without a partner at this session.

4. After about fifteen to twenty minutes call the entire group together. Ask everyone to join hands. Recite an Our Father together. If you have planned a recepion, begin it now. If not, bid everyone farewell.

Appendix

Eight Be-Attitudes for Session Directors

1. Be prepared.

Study the manual carefully. Think through the session plans, outline them, and prepare your own note cards for teaching them. Visualize each activity in your mind, "seeing" it step by step. You should clearly understand the purpose and expected outcome.

2. Be yourself.

Make the material your own. Think about it; pray about it; if possible, talk about it with other adults. Use the ideas in the manual creatively—add your own examples, substitute other activities, shorten or lengthen sections. The sessions should come across to the participants as yours, not as the book's.

3. Be organized.

Have a definite plan of action for each part of a session. Be especially clear about giving directions for discussion exercises and activities. Have all the materials ready for quick distribution.

4. Be flexible.

Be ready to adjust your well-organized plan at a moment's notice. Some activities may last longer or shorter than expected; some won't fit the mood of the evening; some won't work for you or your group. Always have more material planned than you think you will need. Keep your eye on the clock; if you're running short of time, shorten or drop something—but, please, not the Prayer Experience!

5. Be open.

Listen to what the young people have to say, and encourage them to listen to one another. Accept their feelings and ideas even if you don't agree with them. Be ready at times to challenge them (always respectfully) on ideas and positions that are inconsistent, erroneous, or unclear.

6. Be firm.

Do not allow the candidates to be disrespectful of you or to one another. Maintain an orderly, controlled atmosphere even during fun times. Let the young people know that you expect adult conduct from them. (All of this will be made much easier by the presence of adult participants in the group.)

7. Be happy.

Enjoy the young people. Enjoy their nonsense and exuberance as well as their thoughtfulness and serious sharing. Let them know that you like being with them.

8. Be-lieve.

Believe that you aren't in this business alone, that God and the Christian community play active roles in the process of transmitting and sharing faith. Believe that God is involved in the lives of your young people, that the action of God's grace precedes, accompanies, and follows all your efforts. Believe that the faith is alive in your parish community, and that the whole parish is helping in some way to transmit that faith to its youth.

Dialogue: Why and How

The *Developing Faith* series depends on the interaction of the participants for its effectiveness—the interaction of teens with adults and of teens with teens. This interaction is brought about primarily through dialogue. Some of the dialogue in the program is light, fun, humorous. Its purpose is to break down barriers and to build mutual understanding and enjoyment. It also makes serious dialogue possible—serious dialogue in which the teens share with one another their dreams and hopes, their questions and doubts, their values and goals, their faith and prayer.

The dialogue technique is based on several assumptions:

- that faith is an already-present reality in each person, and that dialogue helps to surface, affirm, and strengthen that faith;

- that each person is a source of truth and wisdom, and that the truth of each individual is meant for and needed by the entire community;

- that all people, but especially youth, want to open their hearts and share their deepest beliefs and doubts—all they need is listeners who care;

- that talking about the deepest values in one's life helps to clarify and strengthen them for the speaker, that one understands better what one has just tried to explain to another;

- that the faith of the listener is also strengthened by the dialogue process; one of the most powerful ways of alerting a person to the action of God in his or her life is to hear about God's action in the life of another;

- that dialogue creates the common meaning system that enables those who participate in honest dialogue to become a community.

Dialogue of the sort described here can happen only in an atmosphere of openness and trust. To establish such an atmosphere is to a large extent the responsibility of the session director. But it is also true that the dialogue itself creates the atmosphere. Young people learn to share deeply with one another and with adults by doing it. The director's role is to make the doing easy.

Dialoguing Principles

The dialogue activities in this mini-course are designed to encourage sharing. Though each activity uses a slightly different dialogue technique, some general methodological principles apply to all of them:

Pre-response

Give everyone a chance to record his or her response in some way before asking any individual to respond orally. The pre-response might be written, drawn, shown with hand signals, or indicated by body positions. Make the pre-response easy by asking a very specific question with a concrete answer, by providing a sentence starter to be completed, by giving a spread of answers to choose from. This technique gets everyone involved in answering the question, makes it clear that there is a spread of opinion on the answer rather than the one "right" response, and creates the need for an individual to examine a position contrary to other ideas being presented.

Dialogue starter

Make it easy to get the dialogue started by designating the first speaker, often in a humorous way; for example, the person with the curliest hair, the person with the next birthday, the person wearing the baggiest pants. Each person will then take a turn around the circle. The starter designation usually creates a burst of laughter, thus further relaxing the group.

Pass option

Tell the group that the sharing must always be done freely. If at any time a participant is asked a question he or she doesn't know how to answer, or does not want to answer in public, the person simply says "Pass." If participants choose to respond, however, their answers should be as honest as possible. The pass option is, perhaps, the single most powerful technique in creating an atmosphere where open dialogue can happen. Given the choice of either answering honestly or passing, young people almost always choose to answer. But the pass is always there as a safe and easy way out when things get too hot to handle. It is imperative that the pass option be respected by the directors and by all participants.

Gradual deepening

Move the dialogue gradually from light, easy topics to more serious ones. The easier sharing teaches the technique and warms the participants, thus facilitating deeper sharing.

Listening

Help your group see the important role of the listener in the dialogue process. A person is encouraged to share by sensing that someone is really listening. Everyone in the dialogue circle shares in the listening role. It is important for all the members of the group to look at the speaker, to respond facially to what is said, and to ask follow-up questions. The adults should be especially present to each speaker; at the same time the adults will need to be careful not to become the focus toward which all answers are directed.

Dialoguing Activities

Activities which feature dialogue as a central component include the following:

One-on-one

Designate some way for the participants to pair off (for example, choose as a partner someone you haven't talked to this week, choose a partner who is a different generation or sex, choose a partner who was born in the same month as you). Give the participants something specific to think about and allow a moment of thinking time (for example, think about a living person you admire, think about something you consider evil, think about a recent time you knew God was helping you). Designate which partner should share first. Switch partners and repeat with a new topic.

Panel

Select about six participants to be on a panel. Ways of selecting the panel include asking for volunteers, having each circle select its "least shy" person, drawing names from a hat, calling on elected officers, and so on. Dialogue with the panelists in front of the group for twenty minutes or so. Work from a prepared set of questions but be open to the movement of the dialogue. Listen carefully to the responses and ask follow-up questions based on them. Encourage the panelists to respond to one another. Also encourage response and questions from the audience. You may wish to select a second group of panelists half-way through the session. (This method is a good way for the director to demonstrate the dialogue technique for other participating adults.)

Public interview

Ask for a volunteer who would be willing to dialogue with you in front of the entire group. Interview the person about some area of life that is important to him or her. Work from prepared questions but be flexible.

On the spot

Have the participants write their names on small cards. Collect the cards and shuffle them conspicuously. Pick one name from the pack and ask the person picked if he or she is willing to be "on the spot" for a few minutes. If so, ask a few dialogue questions, then pick another name. The person picked may pass altogether, or pass on any question asked. You may want to keep a set of name cards handy so that you can use this technique at a moment's notice.

Chain reaction

Call on one person to share his or her pre-response to a question. Dialogue briefly with the person about the response, then tell the person to select the next responder. Designate in some way who can be picked; for example, you must pick a person from a different group, a person of the opposite sex.

Grouping Tips

You will need some fast, efficient ways of dividing the participants into dialogue circles. The composition of these circles is important for the success of each session. Each group should contain an even distribution of group moderators, visiting adults, males and females, outspoken and shy persons, and so forth. Try as much as possible to separate members of friendship groups, and always separate family members. It is usually better not to allow participants to select their own groups. Some grouping methods are listed in each of the sessions as required. Some other grouping methods are listed below:

Name tags

If you know ahead of time who will be attending the session, you can use the name tags to designate groups. Follow these steps:

1. Before the session make a name tag for each participant, youth and adult.
2. Put the name tags in groups of eight, selecting the kind of distribution you want in each group.
3. Put a group symbol (letter, number, sign) on each name tag in the pack.
4. Put all the tags back in alphabetical order so they will be easy for the participants to pick up.
5. Put a corresponding group symbol at each table. As participants arrive, ask them to find their symbol and sit at the table.

Leadership distribution

Use this method to establish groupings that will last for several sessions or for the entire program. Note that this method takes a while. The grouping itself should not be done during class time, nor in the presence of the group.

In class:

1. Give everyone, adults and youth, three small tally slips (papers about 1" x 2").
2. Ask each person to select three young people in the class who have leadership qualities. Write one name on each paper and fold once. (If the group is large, you may wish to hand out lists with all the names.)
3. Collect the votes.

Privately:

1. Put the votes in piles: all John's votes in one pile, Mary's in another, and so forth. Count the votes.
2. Decide how many groups you will need. If you need seven, for example, select the seven people with the most votes. Put one in each group and name him or her the youth leader of the group. Select the next seven people with the most votes and name them co-leaders. If the leader is a boy, try to have the co-leader be a girl. Continue to distribute the names according to the votes received. Work for a balance of boys and girls.
3. Assign a group moderator for each group.

4. List all the names for future reference. Put the names of the youth leader and co-leader at the top of the list, but arrange the other names alphabetically so that the persons receiving the least votes will not appear last.

Make use of the leaders in various ways throughout the program. Give them responsibility in planning, making decisions, and so on.

Friendship-group distribution

Use this method if you want to establish grouping for a longer session such as a retreat, or for several sessions. It will also work for one session.

1. As the participants arrive, invite them to sit at tables wherever they choose. They will sit with their natural friendship groups.
2. Give out small cards, one to each person, and ask everyone to write first and last names on the card.
3. Collect the cards yourself, being careful to keep together the cards of people who are sitting together.
4. Decide how many groups you will need (for example, seven). Deal the cards into seven piles as follows. Begin with adults. Then distribute the cards of the boys; then of the girls. The people who were sitting together will automatically end up in different groups.

Parallel lines

This is a fast, easy method for dividing up a very large group, especially if you have no way of knowing beforehand how many people to expect.

1. Estimate the highest number of participants you could logically expect for the session (for example, 160). Divide that number by eight to determine how many groups you might have (for example, twenty). Set up circles of chairs with eight chairs in each. Number the circles from one to twenty.
2. As the participants arrive, have them sign in, adults on one paper, youth on another. Number the papers for easy counting.
3. When all have assembled, check the sign-in sheets to see the total number present and divide by eight to determine how many groups you will actually need. (If it's more than twenty, run for more chairs!)
4. Determine what kind of distribution you want in each group; for example, men, women, boys, girls. Ask the participants to form four parallel lines: men, women, boys, girls.
5. Stand in front of the four lines. Skim off the first four across and send them to circle one; send the second four to circle two; the next four to circle three; and so on until you reach the total number of circles that you need. Half-way down the lines you will begin again with circle one.
6. As you near the end, the lines will be uneven. Fill in the shorter lines from the longer ones.
7. Check to see if any group contains two members of one family. If so, ask one of the family members to switch places with someone of the same age and sex in another group.

Count off

This is the old standby for grouping. Its disadvantage is that some young people will conveniently "forget" their number and move to a circle of their choice rather than to the one assigned.

1. Decide how many groups you will need (for example, seven).
2. Go down the row (or around the circle) and ask each person to count off from one to seven. Count off the group moderators first, then the visiting adults, then the youth.
3. Move to the circles one group at a time. Say, for example: "All the one's follow Mr. Jones, all the two's Mrs. Smith, etc. (Moving to one group at a time makes it more difficult for a person to "forget" and go to the wrong group.)

Free choice method

Once in a while allow the participants to choose their own groups. Do this especially for shorter discussion activities of a more personal nature. This works well when the groupings are just two or three people also.

Tear-out Resource Section

Multiple copies of the following pages are needed for the *Jesus, Should I Follow You?* sessions (see the individual sessions for specific instructions on the use of the materials). The pages are perforated for your convenience in copying the materials for distribution during the sessions.

Mentor Interview and Registration Form

Name: ───────────────────────────────────

Address: ─────────────────────────────────

───────────────────────────────────────

Day Telephone: ───────────────── Night Telephone: ─────────────────

Teen's Name: ──────────────────────────────

Relationship: ──────────────────────────────

Comments: ───────────────────────────────

───────────────────────────────────────

───────────────────────────────────────

───────────────────────────────────────

───────────────────────────────────────

───────────────────────────────────────

───────────────────────────────────────

───────────────────────────────────────

───────────────────────────────────────

───────────────────────────────────────

Interviewed by: ─────────────────────────────

Date: ───────────────────────────────────

Jesus Panel Preparation Sheet

Thank you for agreeing to be on our "Jesus Panel." Please be ready to share a few thoughts about how Jesus makes a difference in your life. Read over the following questions to help in your preparation. You may be asked to answer one or more of these questions as part of the discussion.

- How is Jesus involved in my everyday life?

- How do I feel about Jesus?

- When was a time I recognized Jesus in the words or actions of another person?

- How do I communicate with Jesus?

- When did I first come to know Jesus?

- How does Jesus challenge me?

- How is my life different since I chose to follow Jesus?

- What do I find the hardest about being a follower of Jesus?

- What is Jesus asking of me at this time in my life?

- What is the best advice I can offer people my age or slightly younger about following Jesus?

A Conversation with Jesus

Jesus reader: Come after me, and I will make you fishers of men (Mt 4:19).

Mary reader: How can this be? (Lk 1:34).

Jesus reader: Nothing will be impossible for God (Lk 1:37).

Simon Peter reader: Master, we have worked hard all night and have caught nothing (Lk 5:5).

Jesus reader: Do not let your hearts be troubled. You have faith in God; have faith also in me (Jn 14:1).

Levi reader: And leaving everything behind, Levi got up and followed him (Lk 5:28).

Jesus reader: It was not you who chose me, but I who chose you and appointed you to go and bear fruit (Jn 15:16).

Rich man reader: When the young man heard this statement, he went away sad, for he had many possessions (Mt 19:22).

Jesus reader: I have told you this so that my joy might be in you and your joy might be complete (Jn 15:11).

Zacchaeus reader: Behold, half of my possessions, Lord, I shall give to the poor; and if I have extorted anything from anyone I shall repay it four times over (Lk 19:8).

Jesus reader: Today salvation has come to this house . . . the Son of Man has come to seek and to save what was lost (Lk 19:9-10).

James and John reader: Grant that in your glory we may sit one at your right and the other at your left (Mk 10:37).

Jesus reader: Whoever obeys my commandments and observes them is the one who loves me. And whoever loves me will be loved by my Father (Jn 14:21).

Nicodemus reader: How can this happen? (Jn 3:9).

Jesus reader: If you remain in me and my words remain in you, ask for whatever you want and it will be done for you (Jn 15:7).

The two disciples reader: Rabbi, where are you staying? (Jn 1:38).

Jesus reader: Whoever loves me will keep my word, and my Father will love you, and we will come to you and make our dwelling with you (Jn 14:23).

John the Baptist reader: The one who is coming after me is mightier than I. I am not worthy to carry his sandals (Mt 3:11).

Jesus reader: I say to you, whoever believes in me will do the works that I do, and will do greater ones than these (Jn 14:12).

Saul reader: Saul fell to the ground and heard a voice. . . . He said "Who are you?" (Acts 9:4-5).

Jesus reader: I am the way and the truth and the life. No one comes to the Father except through me (Jn 14:6).

Jesus, Allow Me to Introduce Myself

My full name is:

When I was younger (around the first communion years) you probably knew me as a kid who . . .

I've changed since then. Now I'm a person who . . .

I'd like to follow you because . . .

Brain Teasers

Try to solve as many of the following brain teasers as you can.

1. Each of the items listed below represents a familiar word, names, phrase, or saying. For example CCCCCCC should be recognized as "the seven seas." See if you can work out the others.

a. ADO ADO ADO
   ADO 0 ADO
   ADO ADO ADO

b. WORLAMEN

c. E
   M
   A
   R
   F

d. ONHOLEE

e. ONE ANOTHER
   ONE ANOTHER
   ONE ANOTHER
   ONE ANOTHER
   ONE ANOTHER
   ONE ANOTHER

f. MEAL

2. A word or name that is spelled backward the same as it is forward is called a palindrome (i.e.: bib, sees, madam). Listed below are the definitions of five palindromes with the number of letters in each shown in parenthesis. See how many you can guess.

a. a notable achievement (4)

b. 12 hours after midnight (4)

c. males and females (5)

d. pertaining to public affairs (5)

e. a mechanical part that causes rotation (7)

3. Can you recognize words without their "I's"? Below are nine words from which all the I's have been removed. See if you can work out what the words are by putting back the missing I's.

a. BKN
b. DVDNG
c. LLCT
d. NCLNNG
e. LMTNG
f. VSBLTY
g. MSSNG
h. MSSSSPP
i. TMDTY

From the book: *Brainteasers and Mindbenders* by Ben Hamilton. © copyright 1981. Used by permission of the publisher, Prentice Hall Press/ A Division of Simon and Schuster.

Scripture Cards

Directions: Cut on the dashed lines. Give one card to each of four small groups.

- -

Scripture Card 1
Scripture: John 11:1-44
Directions: When it is your group's turn to present this passage, the first person takes the bible and reads Jesus' words in Jn 11:25-26: "I am the resurrection and the life; whoever believes in me, even if he dies, will live, and everyone who lives and believes in me will never die. Do you believe this?" Then, the person passes the bible to the next person who reads the exact same words. Continue until everyone in the group has read the same passage. Feel free to read in a monotone or exaggerate the "boredom" of hearing the same words over and over.

- -

Scripture Card 2
Scripture: John 4:1-42
Directions: Divide your group into pairs. Each pair should have a small paper cup. Fill the cup with water. When it's your group's turn to present this passage, one person in each pair should silently exchange the cup of water with the other. The person who receives the water should offer a gesture of thankfulness (bow, curtsy, etc.). Then the next pair repeats the same action.

- -

Scripture Card 3
Scripture: John 13:1-20
Directions: Select a good reader to read the entire passage. As the passage is being read, the rest of the group enacts or pantomimes the roles being described. Choose one person to be Jesus. The rest of the group members can be the disciples whose feet are washed.

- -

Scripture Card 4
Scripture: Mark 2:1-12
Directions: Your group is to do a skit to reprise this entire passage. Divide up the roles as narrator, Jesus, the paralytic, the four men who carried him, scribes (vs. 7), and all (vs. 12). Feel free to ad-lib the words and create the scene in the way you wish.

- -

The Big Pay-Off Tally Sheet

Directions: For each round, circle either an A or a B in the space marked choice. Tally your own balance after each round.

Round	Choice (A or B)	$Won	$Lost	Balance
1	A B			
2	A B			
3	A B			
4*	A B			
5	A B			
6*	A B			
7	A B			
8*	A B			

*Bonus rounds (values doubled)

Conversion Speaker Preparation Sheet

Thank you for agreeing to speak to our teens about an experience of personal conversion. In our session we are discussing how anything that is worthwhile involves commitment and sacrifice. In your talk, please include the following as they apply:

- The commitment you are striving to keep.

- What led you to make this commitment

- What experience in your life would you consider a "conversion"?

- The cost of your commitment: something you have to "give up" in order to keep this commitment.

- The rewards there are in keeping this commitment.

- In what sense has the "old" you "died" and in what sense do you now have "new life"?

- How does your commitment to a new life relate to Jesus' call to "pick up your cross" in order to gain new life?

The time allotted for your talk is twenty minutes. If you wish, part of the time can be reserved for questions and answers.